CHRONICLES OF AN OLD INN

CHRONICLES OF AN OLD INN

ANDRÉE HOPE

ISBN: 978-93-5614-099-8

Published: 1887

LECTOR HOUSE LLP
E-MAIL: lectorpublishing@gmail.com

CHRONICLES OF AN OLD INN

OR,
A FEW WORDS ABOUT GRAY'S INN

BY

ANDRÉE HOPE

1887

DEDICATED
BY PERMISSION, AND WITH THE DEEPEST RESPECT,
TO
HIS ROYAL HIGHNESS
THE DUKE OF CONNAUGHT,
𝔗reasurer,
AND TO THE
HONOURABLE SOCIETY OF BENCHERS
OF GRAY'S INN.

PREFACE.

It is with feelings of much diffidence, even with alarm, that this little book is given to the world. It was written to give pleasure to many dear to the writer's heart, relatives and friends, most of whom have already gone to that "Shadowy Land" to which we are all so fast hastening.

They, alas! can no longer feel an interest in the pages written in hours of much happiness and of cruel sorrow. Probably the literary world, of whom the writer stands in trembling awe, will regard with the same indifference a little work so crude and incomplete. But as sometimes a rough sketch brings persons and places as vividly to remembrance as highly finished pictures, perhaps these "In Memoriam Chronicles of an Old Inn" may, in some degree, interest those who have not time to read more skilfully written but longer histories.

CONTENTS

CHRONICLES OF AN OLD INN;
OR,
A FEW WORDS ABOUT GRAY'S INN.

GRAY'S INN.

About half-way down the great thoroughfare of Holborn, there is an old and somewhat gloomy gateway. That gateway is low and dark, but rarely silent, as from early dawn until late into the night it echoes and re-echoes with the thunder of the mighty traffic of the great street on which it opens.

From early dawn until late into the night may be heard the heavy roll of omnibuses, the sharp rattle of cabs, the hurried steps of vast multitudes of foot passengers.

Like the arteries of the living body, that as long as life endures receives fresh blood from the heart, are the main streets that lead from "the City," that heart of gigantic London; and from this great centre of the trade of Europe, the wondrous stream of commerce is for ever flowing.

Of these magnificent streets few are more striking to the stranger than the grand old thoroughfare of Holborn.

Its width, its length, the precipitous hill over which it passes, the noble viaduct that now eases the too rapid descent, the memories that are connected with this, one of the most ancient, as well as one of the most important streets of the English capital, render it more than ordinarily interesting to the foreigner, and to the stranger.

A few of the ancient houses are still in existence, and from their quaint old casements many royal pageants and many sorrowful processions have been witnessed.

Kings and Queens arrayed in gorgeous robes, blazing with costly jewels, and surrounded by glittering courtiers, have gaily moved onwards amid the blare of trumpets, and the shouts of admiring crowds, to partake of sumptuous Court festivals.

In awe-inspiring contrast to the gay trains, and to the beauty and mirth of the pleasure-seekers so joyously riding forward to fresh delight, other scenes have, alas! been too frequently witnessed from these same windows.

Amid the derisive cries of a savage rabble, or amid the gloomy silence of a suffering and oppressed people, other and ghastly processions have also passed this way.

Merciless guards and black-robed priests are here, and in their midst, watched with zealous and cruel care, are tottering and emaciated figures—martyrs on their way to Smithfield, prepared to seal by their blood the testimony they have borne to the truth of their faith.

Broken down by suffering, with a frame ofttimes racked by the torture it has undergone, many an heroic heart has still triumphed over the crushed and mangled body, and with uplifted hands and in fervid accents the Christian hero, even amidst the flames, praises God, who permits His faithful servant to testify, though in death, undying love and confidence in his Divine Father.

God be thanked, however, that these hideous old times have long since passed away, and that England is now, by her noble tolerance and enlightened Christianity, doing much to show the world that it is not by cruelty and persecution that our holy religion requires to be upheld.

Oldbourne, as it was called in olden times, was early one of the important thoroughfares in, or rather leading to the City of London, and although the traffic must in days of yore have been but a faint shadow of what it now is, still even as far back as the reign of Richard II. it was necessary to make special laws for its good ordering, by reason of the number of carts, wains, drays, and other conveyances that passed that way.

One old chronicler complains thus quaintly:

"The coachman rides behind his horses' tails," saith he, "he lasheth them, but looketh not before nor behind him. The drayman sitteth and sleepeth on his dray, and so letteth his horses lead him home."

For the better maintenance of safety, it seems that it had been ordered that the fore horse of every carriage should be led by hand; but we see that in old days, as indeed is sometimes the case now, such prudent regulations were but little regarded. So the same old chronicler mournfully adds: "These wise laws are not faithfully observed."

In these same old days coaches were unknown, but a singular kind of chariot, or large covered chair, slung upon wheels, and called a whirlicote, was used by ladies of high rank.

When Richard II. travelled from Kent to London, the King and all his Court rode on horseback, but the Queen Mother, being weak and sickly, made the journey in a whirlicote.

A new fashion came in vogue the following year, when King Richard married Princess Anne of Bohemia.

The fair young Queen made her first appearance in public arrayed in white robes embroidered in silver, so that "she shone in beauty and brightness like unto a sweet crescent moon," and to the admiration of all beholders, she rode gallantly at the King's left hand, seated sideways on her horse, on a machine called a side-saddle.

From that moment whirlicotes went out of fashion, and every woman who was young enough to mount a horse rode sideways like the Queen.

But centuries have passed away, each century, each year indeed, adding to the mighty stream of traffic, and now the roar of passing vehicles, the hurrying footsteps of thousands of foot passengers, cease not from early dawn until late into the night.

To the unaccustomed ear, to the unaccustomed eye, such overpowering noise, such perpetual movement, speedily becomes bewildering and even stupefying. Ear and eye alike are exhausted by the unwonted strain.

Very few, however, of the many who pass and repass that way, notice the low, dark archway already mentioned opening on the left-hand side of the street when proceeding towards the City. Turn down that archway, and ere twenty steps are made a different world is found. Not only indeed a different world, but a chance visitor might say with reason that he is out of the world, the sudden quiet, the sudden peace, is in such extraordinary contrast to the rush and hurry of the street he has left.

Instead of the blinding glare, the suffocating dust, the bewildering noise of Holborn, the quiet court to which this archway leads, rests in almost monastic calm. Lofty houses intercept the burning rays of the sun, and cast their soft gray shadows half across the square. Even the noise of the great street is softened to the ear, and becomes almost soothing, as the echoes of it fall and are gradually lost amid the thick old walls.

The maddening hubbub of carts, cabs, and hurrying feet fades into an indistinct murmur, like the throbbing of the waves of the great Atlantic when heard far away inland.

To one given to idle and desultory wanderings, and to idle and desultory thoughts, the quaint old nooks and corners that may often be found in the midst even of the most populous towns, have far more charms than the busier haunts of men, for to those who love to muse on bygone days there is a strange and constantly increasing fascination in the conventual quiet, the faded grandeur of many of these time-worn spots.

In truth, however, the old squares of that ancient Inn of Court called Gray's Inn, though quiet and retired, are by no means gloomy. Not only are they cool and restful in the glowing days of summer, but in their pleasant courts some remains may still be found of the sweet country sights, of the sweet country sounds that centuries ago made the drives and walks by Oldbourne Hill, with its pretty lanes and paths, and its fragrant hedgerows, the favourite resort, not only of the tired and heated citizens of London, but also of the great lords whose stately palaces were either grouped around Westminster, or stretched far along the picturesque river-bank then, as now, called the Strand.

No doubt the beautiful and rapidly flowing river had many charms, and we know from Pepys, that during the summer heats its broad bosom was covered with pleasure-boats and wherries.

In those days smoke did not darken, nor did evil smells and sights defile the waters of the sweet Thames. Fair gardens then bordered its banks, and trees and flowers dipped tendrils and branches into its waves.

Still, notwithstanding these attractions, the Londoners dearly loved Old-bourne Hill, where the fresh cool breezes came from the Kent and Surrey hills laden with the sweet scent of gorse and broom (that favourite badge of our Plantagenet Princes), and from the valleys and sunny slopes below came the richer perfumes of innumerable vineyards and hop-grounds.

It is difficult to realise, while wandering amongst the wilderness of houses that now surrounds and connects the cities of London and Westminster, that once fair fields and shady woods extended for miles, where now are only found grimy streets and dismal courts. Still more difficult is it to believe that within the last hundred years these same fair fields were dangerous to traverse after dark, by reason of the many footpads who infested the neighbourhood.

Beyond St. Pancras Church a bell was rung at stated hours, in order that foot passengers who wished to cross the meadows towards Hampstead and Highgate, or go to those suburbs called Camden and Somers Towns, should have the protection of an armed watchman. In those days few persons ventured abroad after nightfall without carrying some defensive weapon. Without gas, without police, London streets as well as London suburbs were fraught with danger.

Now, when dazzled by the glare of the streets, when wearied by the overpowering noise of the great town, a shady corner in quiet Gray's Inn Square seems doubly attractive.

The bright August sun shines fiercely on the opposite pavement. Its rays glint up and down the façade of the tall houses, here and there catching the angle of a projecting cornice, then reddening and almost beautifying some old smoke-blackened chimney.

Many are the beautiful though rarely-noticed spots of colour these rays bring to light.

Tiny atoms of green moss, and of those other hardy lichens that time gathers round about old tiles, glow like gems when caught by the flickering beams. Even the shade-loving lycopodiums, that as years roll on, softly carpet with their minute sprays all the damp, ugly spots into which the sun rarely penetrates, even these modest plants grow brighter and more beautiful as the unwonted warmth and sunshine steal into their secluded corners. With what delicacy and grace does not Nature soften and re-colour all the injuries that time and man's neglect so surely bring about!

As the hours wear on, the restfulness of the old precincts grows more and more sweet. The subdued roar of the great city rises and falls in measured cadence, and mingles quite pleasantly with the cawing of the rooks as they slowly wing their way home from their feeding grounds near Hampstead and Highgate, wheeling and cawing lazily as they circle round the old trees ere they settle themselves for the night.

An ancient rookery still exists in the gardens of the Inn, and the soft evening air, as it sways to and fro the branches of the tall elms in which the nests have been built, brings with it the delicious scent of newly-cut grass.

Well may the Benchers love their Inn. In no other place in London are there so many pleasant reminders of the fair country that once surrounded these Courts and Halls.

When seated in the gardens under the shade of the ancient trees, listening to the songs and chirpings of innumerable birds, it seems really incongruous that in so restful a spot, where so much speaks of quiet country life, weighty legal matters are for ever being transacted. Could we penetrate into the secrets of many of the old, dark houses that frown around, what tales of anxiety, of suffering, what histories of the trials that blight men's lives would come to light.

To the doctor and to the lawyer the deadly malady, the heart-crushing anxiety, must ever be told without reserve. No cruel symptom, no ugly detail, must be concealed. No man may keep a secret from such advisers. Lawyers as well as doctors must be told not only the truth, but the whole often hateful truth.

These old houses could indeed tell many mysterious, many marvellous tales, but silent as they are, their heavy, solid doorways, their long, narrow windows, their broad staircases and lofty rooms, are in themselves a history of the past. They are accurate though mute evidences of the time when they came into being. A faded grandeur still hangs about them, for they were built when land was not sold by the foot as it now is, and space was then a luxury comparatively easily purchased. So the staircases are broad, and the rooms large and lofty; but years have passed, centuries have passed, and staircases and passages have grown dusky and dim, and the handsome rooms devoted only to the stern purposes of life, and uncheered or graced by the softening presence of woman, have become shabby and harsh of aspect. So generation after generation of lawyers dwell here and pass away, each generation leaving an additional shadow of dusky shabbiness upon the poor old rooms.

The occupiers of the Inn are for the most part day dwellers only, doing their work in chambers, and leaving in the evening for their houses elsewhere.

Some few bachelors, however, make their home here, and when that is the case, the sets of chambers so occupied are the perfection of comfort. Those who have the good fortune to know these snug abodes, may well be eloquent as to their merits. The solid old mahogany tables, the exquisitely finished Chippendale chairs, are mellow with age, and glow with the rich gloss produced by much rubbing. Then the fireplaces, so hospitably deep and ample, where the ruddy flames can so well be seen as they dart up the great chimneys, casting their light upon the quaint masks and carvings that adorn the mantel-shelves; they make the ugly faces laugh as they are caught by the genial light.

The roomy arm-chairs, too, have assumed the cosy hollowness that speaks of constant use, and look most invitingly comfortable.

During summer the long narrow windows will be opened upon the bright and sunny garden, where great beds of mignonette and long lines of sweet-peas make the summer air full of fragrance; and not unfrequently on a warm, drowsy afternoon may be heard the soothing tones of a violoncello played by no unskilful hand, and perchance a tender old melody of Purcell or Glück, or one of the grand harmonies of Beethoven, adds yet another charm to the peace and restfulness of the place.

In short, in many parts of this pleasant Inn old age has attained that judicious number of years when men wisely discard mere show, and are content to seek and obtain intense comfort.

Some of the residents in Gray's Inn are Benchers, and these gentlemen are not only entitled to chambers, but during Term time an especial dinner is provided for them in the Great Hall; and as the Society always numbers amongst its members some of the most distinguished men of the day, it may readily be understood how interesting and attractive these meetings are.

Inns of Court were originally so called because the students belonging to them were bound to attend and serve the Courts of Judicature.

Anciently these colleges received none but the sons of noblemen, and of those gentlemen whose rank qualified them to do service to the King in his Court.

Fortescue affirms that in his time there were about two thousand students in the Inns of Court and of Chancery, all of whom were *filii nobilium*, or gentlemen born. But the rigidity of this rule was gradually relaxed, and in the reign of Queen Elizabeth, Sir Edward Coke reckons that not more than half the students then studying in the various Inns were of gentle birth.

These Inns of Court, that for centuries have been so justly famed for the education and introduction of men of learning in the law, are governed by masters, principals, Benchers, stewards, treasurers, and other officers.

Amongst their buildings are public halls for exercises, such as reading, declaiming, reciting, etc. At one time every student was compelled to attend and take part in these exercises for a certain number of years before he was admitted to plead at the Bar. At the present day, however, most of these regulations have fallen into disuse, and are no longer insisted upon.

The societies have not any judicial authority over their members, but they have certain orders and rules amongst themselves, which have by consent the force of laws.

For slight offences persons are excommoned, or put out of commons. For graver faults they forfeit their chambers, or, indeed, may be expelled the college. When an offender has been thus expelled, he can never be received by any of the other societies.

The members of these societies, or Inns, may be divided into Benchers, outer barristers, inner barristers, and students.

The Inns themselves are divided into, and are severally denominated, Inns of Chancery and Inns of Court.

The most ancient of the former is Thavies Inn, which was begun in the reign of Edward III. The other Inns of Chancery are New Inn, Symond's Inn, Clement's Inn, Clifford's Inn (once the property of Lord Clifford), Staples' Inn (so called because it had belonged to the Merchants of the Staple), Lion Inn (formerly an ordinary hostelry for travellers, bearing the sign of the Lion), Furnival's Inn, and Barnard's Inn.

Inns of Chancery were, in the earlier centuries, considered as a preparatory college for the younger students, who could here pursue the studies that would enable them to be admitted into the Inns of Court.

The four principal Inns of Court are the Inner Temple, the Middle Temple, Lincoln's Inn, and Gray's Inn.

Gray's Inn formerly belonged to Lord Gray, and Lincoln's Inn to the Earl of Lincoln. The Inner and Middle Temple, once the dwellings of the famous Knights Templar, were purchased about three hundred years ago by the then leading Professors of the Common Law.

There are also two other Inns, those of the Serjeants of the Law.

The general daily life in the Inns of Court during olden times, is described by Fortescue with much minuteness, and appears to have been both varied and attractive:

"On working days most of the students applied themselves to the study of the law, and on holy days to the study of Holy Scripture. At the same time, however, the students were not allowed to neglect lighter pursuits, for they learned to sing, and to exercise themselves in all kind of harmony, and they also made provision for the exercise and consequent health of the body, for they constantly practised dancing and other noblemen's pastimes. They did everything in peace and amity."

This last assertion appears somewhat startling in an age when scenes of brawling and fighting were of almost daily occurrence in the streets of London. However, it may be presumed that in these old times the heads of societies, having young men to take care of, did try to take care of them, and did not leave them quite so much to themselves as is the case in these modern days.

No doubt, there is much to be said in favour of training boys, as early as possible, to be self-dependent.

We are proud, and proud with reason, of "Our Boys." Still the most sanguine amongst us must admit that there is room for improvement in the system that is adopted in most of our schools and colleges.

It is the fashion now to deem that old heads can be seated on very young shoulders. These young fellows, scarcely more than children in years, are left to their own guidance, both morally and physically.

We may indeed glory in our boys in many respects. They are manly, honourable, brave, and truthful, with a truthfulness that makes many a parent's heart beat high with pride and pleasure; and yet, in how many households has not the sad knowledge come that the boys so loved, so gloried in, are ignorant and selfish—ignorant of most of the branches of useful knowledge, having tacitly been permitted to adopt habits of grievous self-indulgence?

When the young fellow has to enter upon his profession, when he has really

to fight the battle of life, how often is it not found that the expensive education bestowed upon him (often at the cost of much self-denial from the rest of the family)
is worth absolutely nothing?

Now that the fruit of so much learning has to be gathered, it is discovered that
there is actually no fruit to gather; that, in order to be eligible even for the contest
of these competitive examinations, a young man who has been at school for years
has to learn the very rudiments of necessary knowledge, and must *cram* himself in
a few months, and at a dire expenditure of money and health, in those very subjects that he has so long been *nominally* studying.

In how few schools are writing, English composition, arithmetic, geography,
or modern languages thoroughly taught? And yet these are the very subjects absolutely essential for a candidate in a competitive examination.

Then again, with regard to those who study hard. How many and how sad are
the cases where the student has broken down physically, because due care had not
been taken of the bodily health, while the brain had been unduly taxed?

There are, doubtless, exceptional instances of genius so marvellous that work
comes easily both to mind and body. These are the men who become eventually
our great statesmen, our great lawyers; but these mighty ones are the exception,
not the rule. Few, indeed, are they whose talents and whose powers enable them
to overcome every difficulty.

For the most part the learned student sinks into a frail and over-sensitive man,
whose weak physical strength breaks down under a too severe mental strain. Often, indeed, it does so on the very eve of victory.

One of the most touching, and yet one of the truest and most vivid pictures
ever given to us by that great writer Bulwer, is the sorrowful story in "Pelham" of
the gentle and learned scholar, a student so skilled in book learning that he had
distanced all his compeers of the day, and yet so feeble in health, so deficient in
what is called common-sense, that he was incapable of ruling his own household,
or of coping with the every-day affairs of life.

Surely there must be some means by which those appointed to rule can exercise a discreet supervision over the boys and young men entrusted to their care. A
supervision which, while not entrenching on their liberty, will yet lead into right
ways those who are entering on the varied and dangerous paths of life.

Some wise writer has said: "More education is effected during the *amusements*
of youth than is gained by all the *studies* to which teachers give such zealous care."

Now, in most places where boys are being trained, it seems a point of honour
that out of school the masters shall never interfere, nor, indeed, in most cases do
they appear.

Besides the practices of olden times already mentioned the ancient custom
called "Moots" must not be forgotten.

Gray's Inn was especially conspicuous for those exercises, which Stow calls

"Boltes," "Mootes," or "putting of cases," for the "Boltes" were conversational arguments addressed to or put to a student by a Bencher and two barristers in private.

Subsequently, when the student had become a sufficiently expert "Bolter," he was admitted to the "Mootes," where questions upon legal matters were debated by the students in the presence of the Benchers of the Society.

The object of these exercises was to promote the faculty of ready speaking, and, in order to secure this end, the disputants were kept in ignorance of the topic to be argued until called upon to discuss it.

The case, drawn up by the Reader, was laid upon the salt-cellar before meals; none were permitted to look into it under pain of expulsion from the Society.

These discussions were strictly legal, and the proceedings were conducted as nearly as possible in like manner to those of the Courts themselves. "About the end of the 17th century," says Lord Campbell, "Mootes fell into disuse, and they have now entirely ceased."

It is in such institutions as these Inns of Court and other similar communities, that the old feudal feeling respecting ancient servitors has been retained in much of its pristine integrity. Many of the old servants and inferior officers of Grays Inn may be said to belong to the place by right of descent. They were born within its precincts, they have been trained beneath the shadows of its old walls. In their youth they began their course of serving under the guidance of father, or grandfather, and now, in their old age, have in their turns some post of trust and responsibility confided to them.

There is something especially delightful and heart-stirring in the service of gray-headed men who have passed their lives in the same place, serving the same masters.

Shakespeare felt this, when, in describing old Adam in *As You Like It*, he makes the old man say:

> Master, go on, and I will follow thee,
> To the last gasp, with love and loyalty.

Most of the old servitors in Gray's Inn are well-educated, well-informed men, and are in general fully acquainted with the histories, traditions, and quaint biographies connected with the ancient Courts wherein their lives have been passed.

The chief objects of their pride and affection, are of course the Benchers. For the Benchers they entertain the profound reverence that so powerful a body of learned men is entitled to expect, and this respect is mingled at the same time with the affectionate solicitude that old servants have for kind and esteemed masters.

They feel a great interest in the students, although they regard them for the most part as wild young fellows, promising, no doubt, but still far from possessing the talents of former generations of lawyers. They will sometimes, indeed, shake their heads dolefully over the degeneracy of young men of to-day, when compared with the youth of the celebrated personages, whose names adorn the walls of the great hall.

Respecting the old buildings and old customs of the Inn they love to dilate for the hour together, and even the rooks come in for a share of their affection, and also for a considerable amount of anxiety, for this venerable community shows alarming symptoms of decay, the aërial colony having sadly diminished of late years.

In vain has the welfare of the infant progeny been tenderly watched over, latterly many unnatural parent rooks appear to have taken a dislike to their own offspring, and in that case peck the little ones to death without thought of parental duty.

One old gray-headed rook, who is always the first to arrive on the ground when feeding time has come, and who hops about with an uncommonly consequential air, from all accounts appears to be a perfect reprobate among his fellows. The number of wives he has cruelly injured, and the number of children he has kicked out of the nest have acquired for him the evil reputation of being the ringleader of the badly disposed of the feathered tribe.

Unfortunately, also, there is reason to fear that so bad an example has perverted several of the younger husbands and fathers. Infanticide has indeed of late so much increased, that it has now become a matter of grave consideration whether it will not be advisable to inflict the extreme punishment of the law upon the chief criminal. It is feared that it will be necessary to put this venerable gray head to death, as a terrible example to all rooks, and as a warning to all intending sinners.

Unhappily it must be admitted that the diminution of these interesting inhabitants of the higher regions is not altogether owing to their domestic delinquencies. It is, no doubt, partly caused by the rapid growth of London, and the great distance the rooks have now to traverse in order to arrive at their natural feeding grounds.

Another and deplorable cause arises from the decay and unavoidable destruction of some of the oldest trees.

In former years there was a very large rookery in the gardens of Gray's Inn. In 1875, however, storms and severe winters had so broken and damaged many of the largest trees that it was necessary to cut them down. This was done in March, and in April, to the consternation of the inhabitants of the Inn, the rooks departed in a body, as if indignant at being thus despoiled of a portion of their dominions.

For nearly a month not a bird appeared; then about six pair shyly returned, as if unwilling to quit for ever so fair and so peaceful a dwelling.

The other wanderers have never come back; but the little colony, though so much diminished from what it was in days of yore, still flourishes and indeed prospers.

There are more nests this spring than there have been for several past years, and it may therefore be hoped that this ancient rookery may long continue to be one of the charms and attractions of Gray's Inn.

Its existence undoubtedly mainly depends upon the durability of the grand and beautiful dwelling-places of the birds, the noble old elms, and unhappily such old elm trees are dangerous neighbours. With age their wood becomes not only brittle, but peculiarly liable to internal decay.

After the heavy rains that so often succeed dry summers, huge branches, sometimes the tree itself, will fall without warning. Such accidents not unfrequently occur in calm and quiet weather when danger is not suspected; the vicinity of elm trees is therefore perilous to life as well as to neighbouring buildings.

Besides rooks, many other birds, rare to London, may not unfrequently be found in the pleasant gardens of Gray's Inn.

Dun, or hooded crows, have occasionally been seen here, and even jackdaws sometimes come for a meal.

As for the starling, this clever bird knows where he is well off, he is therefore a very constant visitor. Many delicate little songsters too, who, having escaped from their cages, find that the liberty they have gained has only made them persecuted waifs and strays in the wilderness of London, seem to know, by intuition, that here they are not only in safety, but secure of a kind welcome.

Goldfinches, chaffinches, green and gray linnets, the lesser redpole, robins, willow-wren, even the song-thrush may from time to time be found here, and, perched on the lower branches of the trees, reward the kind hands that have given them food by pouring forth some of their sweetest and most touching songs.

During the last three winters the tiny tomtit, with his pretty blue head and delicate yellow breast, has made his appearance, and amongst the rarer visitors are fieldfares, redwings, and the great titmouse.

As for the pert little friendly sparrows, they are evidently aware that this is the land of plenty, so they hop about the old Courts with an assuming air of assured proprietorship; and from house-top, doorsill, and projecting eave, chirp condescending acknowledgments of the good things they enjoy.

But why linger in the old Courts when the soft west wind is murmuring so invitingly amongst the branches of the tall trees? Even the birds cannot remain quiet this bright summer's evening. See how they are flitting in and out the masses of dark green leaves, perching first here, then there, and peeping into every crack and crevice of the old bark. Now, many dart upwards to the topmost branches, whence they pour forth their summer gladness in a burst of joyous song.

Let us go to the pleasant gardens—gardens so pleasant, not only in themselves, but also charming with all the associations of past ages; so connected with the pleasant hours passed here by men both learned and celebrated in our history.

Every ancient tree has its story; every sunny grass-plot could relate a little romance.

How many a love tale has doubtless been told and listened to in these quiet alcoves? How many a courtly dame has gloried in the compliments paid to her beauty when walking on these smooth lawns?

There is every reason to believe that these gardens were designed and laid out in 1597 by Lord Bacon, who was then treasurer of Gray's Inn.

Do we not all know how dearly this great and clever man loved gardens? He says: "God Almighty first planted a garden; and, indeed, it is the purest of human pleasures; it is the greatest refreshment to the spirits of man."

In the accounts of the Inn about that date appear the following items:

"4th July, 1597. Ordered that the summee of £7 15s. 4d. due to Mr. Bacon, for planting of elm trees in the walkes be paid next term;" and again, in the following year, there was an order made for the supply of more young elms, etc., the cost of which, as appears by Mr. Bacon's accounts, was £60 6s. 8d., a very large sum in those days.

We learn also from Howell's "Familiar Letters" and from Pepys' "Diary," that Gray's Inn Walks were at one time a fashionable promenade. Howell, writing from Venice in 1621, to a friend residing in Gray's Inn, says: "I hold your walks to be the pleasantest place about London, and that you have there the choicest society." Pepys seems to have frequently visited Gray's Inn Gardens as appears by his "Diary": "4th May, 1662. When church was done my wife and I walked to Gray's Inn to observe fashions of the ladies, because of my wife's making some clothes."

Cannot we picture to ourselves quiet Mrs. Pepys carefully scanning the gay apparel of the fine ladies as they passed to and fro? daintily walking with the little mincing French step that the fair Lady Castlemaine had brought into fashion? The good little wife absorbed in the many intricacies of plaits and puckers, weighing the several advantages to be obtained by the use of plain or damask stuffs, all unconscious, probably, that her volatile husband was as curiously scanning the black eyes and pretty faces that had such overpowering attractions for his wandering fancy.

Pepys again says:

"17th August, 1662. I was very well pleased with the sight of a fine lady that I have often seen walk in Gray's Inn Gardens."

Dryden, in his "Sir Martin Marall," 1661, makes the following reference to Gray's Inn Walks:

"*Sir John Shallow*. But where did you appoint to meet him?

"*Mrs. Millicent*. In Gray's Inn Walks."

Addison, in the *Spectator*, selects the terrace in Gray's Inn Gardens as the place where Sir Roger de Coverley enjoys his morning walk. He describes the dear old baronet as "hemming twice or thrice to himself with great vigour, for he loves to clear his pipes in good air, to make use of his own phrase, and is not a little pleased with any one who takes notice of the strength which he still exerts in his morning hems."

Charles Lamb, in his delightful "Essays of Elia," gives an interesting description of these gardens, adding, however, an indignant protest against the injury their beauty had received from the ugly pile of houses called Verulam Buildings, that had been recently erected. He says:

"I am ill at dates, but I think it is now better than five-and-twenty years ago that, walking in the gardens at Gray's Inn—they were then finer than they are now—the accursed Verulam Buildings had not encroached upon all the east side of them, cutting out delicate green crankles, and shouldering away one of two of the stately alcoves of the terrace. The survivor stands, gaping and relationless, as if it remembered its brother. They are still the best gardens of any of the Inns of Court—my beloved Temple not forgotten—have the gravest character, their aspect being altogether revered and law-breathing. Bacon has left the impress of his foot upon their gravel walks."

If the gardens give the summer charm to these old precincts, the grand old Hall is the glory, and may well be called the heart of Gray's Inn.

Seventy feet in length, thirty-five in width, and forty-seven in height, it is in truth a stately chamber, yet so harmonious are its proportions, so graceful are its details, that the spectator knows not which to admire most, the simple grandeur of its size, the delicate beauty of the old stained glass windows, or the rich deep colouring that time has given to the oaken panelling as well as to the heavy oaken furniture.

At the east end is a raised daïs, the place of honour, on which stands the table reserved for the Benchers and their guests.

The students dine in the body of the Hall, and the great black oak tables and settles that they use were placed here in the reign of Queen Elizabeth. As they were then, so they are now, and so they may probably remain for as many more hundred years.

In those good or bad old times, wood and labour were of comparatively little value, so furniture was then massive, and often decorated with a lavish richness of detail that a modern upholsterer would dread as much as he would admire, so great would be the modern cost both of the material and the work expended on it. How many remnants of the tables and chairs of this veneering age will there be in another century?

Near the daïs is a great oriel window, that beautiful characteristic of the Tudor period; the old coloured glass, rich with the armorial bearings of the Society, and emblazoned also with names well known and distinguished in our English history.

An elaborately carved oaken screen at the opposite end of the Hall conceals the entrance vestibule, and supports a Minstrel Gallery, another delightful adjunct to the large Halls of the fifteenth and sixteenth centuries.

The screen itself is of quaint but handsome design, and is especially interesting, as its decorations denote the period when it was erected. Short, thick Ionic columns, carved in arabesque with scroll ornaments, are surmounted by a range of semicircular arches. Above these is a balustrade of open carving enclosing the Minstrels' Gallery.

Fortunately restorations have not been needed, nor have alterations been made since the screen was placed here. As years have rolled on, therefore, the solid old oak has acquired that richness of tone and beauty of colouring that time alone can give.

Above the gallery is a large traceried window, and, as on the north and south walls are nine mullioned and transomed windows, the Great Hall is bright, well-lighted, and cheerful.

The great space between windows and floor is oak-panelled, and enriched by the coats of arms of members of the Society who have filled the office of treasurer.

There is something pleasant, but nevertheless sad, in reading over the names of many, honoured in their time, still honoured here in this venerable Inn of Court, but yet how long ago forgotten by the world without.

Forgotten long ago, although as English laws are founded on precedent, and not upon written codes, celebrated English lawyers probably make more mark upon English history than great men of other professions.

In every Government the Lord Chancellor is invariably a member of the Cabinet, and most of our leading statesmen have begun their career by studying, even if they have not practised, the profession of the Law. Still how very many there are, who, famous in their time, have passed away from all men's remembrance, and but for the names inscribed on these parental old walls, have struggled, gained the prize, and yet have again faded into the darkness from which they fought so hard to emerge.

Truly the glory of this world is but a shadow, nought but a faint glimmer of a brief and perishing light.

The fine open roof of the Hall, with its great hammer-beam timbers, is also a grand relic of the past; but the ancient *reredos*, or brass grate which once stood in the centre of the chamber, as well as its *louvre*—or smoke chimney—has been removed, and replaced by a modern stove. A great lapse from beauty, but, nevertheless, a change that contributes much to warmth and comfort.

The exterior of the building has, unhappily, been modernised, and, in accordance with the bad taste that prevailed during the greater part of the last century, the venerable brickwork has been covered with stucco.

It seems extraordinary that this miserable pretence of stone should at one time have been so universally adopted in England, because, while subject to the same discolouration and decay that injure stone in this damp climate, age does not bestow upon it either dignity or rich colouring.

Happily, fine brickwork is now beginning to be appreciated. Not only is it rich in point of colour, but, skilfully used, the most delicate ornamentation can be obtained. Witness, for instance, the glorious old church of San Ambrogio in Milan, and in many churches of towns in North Italy, where bricks have been used without any admixture of stone or marble.

It must not be supposed that the noble and dignified old Hall of Gray's Inn has been used solely for the pleasures of the table.

Many a gay masque, many a joyous revel has been held within its ancient walls.

Royalty itself has frequently honoured by its presence the balls, banquets, marriage feasts, and other "merrie makings" given by the Honourable Society of Gray's Inn.

Queen Elizabeth came here soon after her accession to the throne.

The fair maiden Queen, then in the early bloom of youth, deigned to tread a measure on the floor of the Hall, and her beauty and grace so turned the heads of some of the more impressionable students, that two of them became raving mad from love for their Royal and unapproachable mistress.

Knowing how hopeless their passion was, these luckless young fellows resolved to put themselves to death. They could not endure their cruel torment; like the Persians, they declared their hearts were burnt up with fire, and that life had become but a burden to them.

The legend, however, only relates their sufferings, their struggles, and their desperate purpose. It is silent as to whether these fatal intentions were ever carried into execution. It may be hoped, therefore, that these love-sick youths recovered in time from their love fit. The study of the law does not tend to foster romance, and hard work in most cases is an effectual panacea against the blighting effects of hopeless passion.

Standing in the old Hall, we can see, in fancy, the grand and picturesque entertainment. We can see the young and graceful, though somewhat stern-faced girl, queening it so royally amongst her enthusiastic admirers. How happy she is now in her consciousness of youth, and consequent beauty, in her royal dignity, a Queen at last in her glorious kingdom. Above all, especially happy in being at length free, no longer in daily terror of a prison or a scaffold. No longer dreading to have to seal by her blood her resolve to keep intact her royal position as heir to the throne, safe at last from the terror of being called on to lay down her life ere she would abjure her religion for that of her bigot sister Mary.

No wonder the young Sovereign was then bright and happy.

It is sad to think of the changes that years brought about. It is sad to think of the suspicious, cold-hearted, merciless old woman, signing not only the death warrant of the beautiful cousin of whom she was so jealous, but also the death warrants of the men whom she had professed to love.

Truly it may be said that envy, malice, and uncharitableness are the vices to which the great and prosperous are peculiarly exposed. Greatness and prosperity eventually produce the very whips that scourge those who have not been constantly chastened by care and sorrow; for the Almighty bestows His good gifts far more equally than we mortals can in general either perceive or understand.

There is a peace of heart in lowly stations that the great can but seldom enjoy. The biography of celebrated monarchs and statesmen sufficiently shows that no rank, however exalted, is exempt from mortifications and annoyances, trying alike to temper and to pride, and it is very evident from such histories that the noblest of all governments, the government of oneself, is far more difficult of attainment for the exalted than for the humbler inhabitants of earth.

Not only during Queen Elizabeth's reign, but at a much earlier period, the Inns of Court had been celebrated for the magnificence of their masques and revels.

The first entertainment of this kind, of which there is any certain record, took place at Gray's Inn in the year 1525.

Hall in his chronicle thus speaks of it:

"A Plaie at Gray's Inn. This Christmas was a goodly disguising played at Gray's Inn, which was compiled by John Roo, Serjeant at the Law, twenty years past. This plae was so set forth with rich and costly apparel, and with strange devices of masks and morrisches, that it was highly praised by all men, except by the Cardinal (Wolsey), who imagined the play was devised of him. In a great fury he sent for Master Roo, and took from him his Coif, and sent him to the Fleet, and afterwards he sent for the young gentlemen that played in the play, and highly rebuked and threatened them, and sent one of them, called Master Moyle of Kent, to the Fleet, but by means of friends Master Roo and he were delivered at last.

"This play sore displeased the Cardinal, and yet it was never meant for him; wherefore many wise men grudged to see him take it so to heart; and even the Cardinal said the King (Henry VIII.) was highly displeased at it, and spake nothing of himself."

This unfortunate play seems to have made a great stir at the time, for not only Hall, but Fox, in his "Acts and Monuments," thus alludes to the performance when writing of a certain Simon Fish, who also belonged to Gray's Inn. Fox says:

"It happened the first year this gentleman came to London to dwell, which was about the year of our Lord, 1525, that there was a certain play, or interlude, made by one M. Roo, of the same Inn, gentleman, in which play partly was matter against the Cardinal Wolsey; and when none durst take upon them to play that part which touched the said Cardinal, this aforesaid Mr. Fish took upon him to do it. Whereupon great displeasure ensued against him on the Cardinal's part, insomuch as he, being pursued by the said Cardinal the same night that this tragedy was played, was compelled of force to avoid his own house, and so fled over the sea to Tindal."

It is singular that neither Hall nor Fox makes any mention of the name of the play that had such unhappy results for the luckless gentlemen who took part in it.

The powerful Cardinal was a dread enemy. He brooked neither insult nor slight, and, when angered, was apt to carry out his vengeance with a completeness that, at the least, brought ruin on his victims. Happy indeed were they did they escape with their lives.

The two offenders on this occasion paid a heavy price for their night's amusement. Their professional prospects were destroyed for ever, their names were erased from the list of Gray's Inn, and never again appeared on it. To Roo, a Serjeant in the Law of twenty years' standing, such a penalty must have been a cruel blow.

Hard work seems to have been seasoned with much amusement in the merry days of Queen Bess, for at no period do we read of so many masques, revels, and such like entertainments as during the reign of our maiden Queen.

Men of all ages and ranks, even those devoted to the learned and severe study of the law, indulged themselves to the full in these amusements. Judges and statesmen condescended to arrange and fashion the festivities, and occasionally indeed took part in them, nothing daunted by the fact that they not unfrequently ended in brawls and fighting. Men fought fiercely too in these turbulent times, and the arms then in common use were formidable weapons. It was the custom to carry bucklers with a point or poke, as it was called, in the centre, from ten to twelve inches in length. Every haberdasher sold these bucklers, and their use became so much abused, that, in the eighth year of Elizabeth, a proclamation was issued prohibiting the sale of any of which the poke exceeded two inches in length. At the same time, the length of swords was limited to one yard and half a quarter, nor was any dagger to have a blade above twelve inches long.

In the records we have respecting many of these gay doings and magnificent festivals, Gray's Inn and the Temple appear to have taken the lead, and at last a sort of union was entered into between the two Inns. Over the great gates of the gardens of the Inner Temple appears the "Griffin" of Gray's Inn, whilst over the principal entrance in Gray's Inn Square, is carved in bold relief the "Winged Horse" of the Inner Temple.

A curious pamphlet, published in 1594, commemorates this union. It is entitled, "Gesta Grayorium, or the History of the High and Mighty Prince, Henry Prince of Purpoole, etc."

It gives a very detailed account of a grand masque that took place on the 20th December, with a minute description of the rich and quaint costumes worn by the actors who took part therein.

There is reason to think that Lord Bacon himself organised this revel, and also assisted in its preparation.

On the said 20th December, it being St. Thomas's Eve, the Prince of Purpoole, as he is termed (Purpoole being the name of the property on which Gray's Inn was built), accompanied by a long train of courtiers and followers, marched in procession from his lodgings in the Inn to the Great Hall, where all things had with fitting dignity been prepared for his reception.

Here he seated himself on a magnificent throne, having over his head a canopy made of rich cloth of state. His great Lords and Councillors grouped themselves around him. Below the daïs were seated his learned council and his learned lawyers, while the numerous officers and attendants of his Court were arranged becomingly in their proper places.

The narrator dilates with much enthusiasm on the magnificence and beauty of the spectacle, and we can well believe the effect must have been fine. Still, in these prosaic days, we find it difficult to understand the Lord High Chancellor and the Queen's Judges of the High Court of Justice giving much thought and time to an entertainment of this description.

However, there is no doubt that in these same riotous, fighting, turbulent, and yet romantic times such spectacles did excite prodigious interest. Our chronicler continues to relate, that common report had so cried up the merits of this especial performance, that the expectation of strangers, both English and foreign, was greatly excited, insomuch that it became necessary to repeat it, and to have many grand nights especially arranged for the entertainment of distinguished strangers.

Unhappily however, then, as is sometimes the case now, the crowd of spectators greatly exceeded the space provided for their accommodation. The multitude of beholders, indeed, was so considerable that there was not convenient room for those who were actors. Many of the performers among the Templarians (as they were then called) left the Hall so displeased and angry that their discontent resulted in blows, and the fighting became so furious that the next day it was found necessary to have an inquiry into the cause of "these disorders."

Nothing daunted, however, by the ill-success of their opening night, the revellers organised another grand performance on the 3rd January following, in honour of a great number of ambassadors, knights, ladies, and other worshipful personages, amongst whom were the Lord Keeper, the Lords Shrewsbury, Burleigh, Cumberland, most of the officers of State and of the Queen's household, and it is said all these guests had convenient places and very good entertainment.

The Temple and Gray's Inn were now reconciled and had become friendly again, so the day after this entertainment the Prince of Purpoole, accompanied by the "Ambassadors of Templaria," and attended by eighty gentlemen of Gray's Inn and the Temple (each of them wearing a plume on his head), dined in state with the Lord Mayor at Crosby Place.

The next grand night was upon Twelfth Night, on which occasion there was again a great company of lords, ladies, and knights; and at Shrovetide the Prince and his company visited Queen Elizabeth at Greenwich.

After the performance Her Majesty "willed the Lord Chamberlain that the gentlemen should be invited on the next day, and that he should present them to her," which was done, and Her Majesty gave them her hand to kiss, with most gracious words of commendation to them, "particularly and in general of Gray's Inn, as an house that she was much beholden unto, for that it did always study for some sports to present unto her."

The same night there was fighting at "Barriers," at which the Prince behaved so valiantly and skilfully that the prize, a jewel set with seventeen diamonds and four rubies, was presented to him by the Queen.

The following order of Pension, to defray the expenses of the above entertainment, was made on February 9th, 37th Elizabeth.

"At this Pension it is ordered that every Reader of this House, towards the charges of the shows and sports before Her Majesty at Shrovetide last year, shall pay ten shillings, and every Ancient six shillings and eightpence, and every Utter Barrister five shillings, and every other Gentleman of this Society, three shillings and sixpence before the end of this term."

There is a tradition in Gray's Inn that the screen already mentioned under the gallery in the Great Hall, as well as the dining tables now used in the Hall, were given to the Society by that Queen as tokens of Her Majesty's regard.

Queen Elizabeth's memory is still held in much affection by the ever loyal subjects in Gray's Inn, and on the Grand Day of each term "the glorious, pious, and immortal memory of good Queen Bess" is still solemnly given in Hall.

In 1613, "the Maske of Flowers was presented by the Gentlemen of Graie's Inn, in the Banqueting House, at the Court of Whitehall, on the occasion of the marriage of the Earle of Somerset with the Lady Frances, daughter of the Earl of Suffolk."

In "The Court and Times of King James I.," there is a letter from I. Chamberlaine, dated 23rd December, 1613, in which he says:

"Sir Francis Bacon prepares a masque to honour their marriage which will stand him in above £2,000, and, although he has been offered some help by the House, and especially by Mr. Solicitor Sir Henry Yelverton, who would have sent him £500, yet he would not accept it."

The story of this masque was published the following year, with a dedication "to the verie honourable Sir Francis Bacon, His Majesty's Attorney-General."

The dedication states:

"That you have graced in general the Societies of the Innes of Court in continuing them still as third persons with the nobility and Court, in doing the King honour, and particularly Graie's Inne, which, as you have formerly brought to flourish both in the ancienter and younger sort by countenancing virtue in every quality, so now you have made a notable demonstration thereof in the lighter and less serious kind."

The members of this learned Society did not always, it appears, amuse themselves in so discreet a manner, for there is a letter in the same book, "The Court and Times of James I.," relating that:

"The gentlemen of Gray's Inn, to make an end of Christmas, on Twelfth Night, at the dead time of the night, shot off all the chambers (small cannon), which they had borrowed from the Tower, being as many as filled four carts.

"The King, awakened by this noise, started out of his bed, and cried: 'Treason! treason!' So the City was in an uproar, in such sort, as it is said, that the whole Court was raised, and almost in arms, the Earl of Arundel running to the bed-chamber, with his sword drawn, as to rescue the King's person."

The following sketch of a ticket of admission to the masque at Gray's Inn on the 2nd February, 1682, is taken from Nichol's "Progresses of Elizabeth:"

This entertainment is thus alluded to by Luttrell in his diary:

"On Saturday the 4th inst., the revells began at Graie's Inn. On 23rd January, Sir Richard Gipps, master of the revells at Graie's Inn, attended by his revellers and comptrollers, went to Whitehall in one of His Majesty's coaches, with several noble men's coaches, and six horses, to invite the King and Queen, the Duke (York) and Duchesse, and the rest of the Court, to a mask at Graie's Inn, on Candlemas Day; and accordingly there was great preparation that day, diverse of the nobility and gentry in masks attended, who danced in the Hall, and afterwards were entertained with a splendid banquet."

Evelyn had already spoken of these revels in terms of contempt and disapprobation, terming them "solemn fooleries," and regretting that the King countenanced them and the deep play that usually concluded the evening. He says:

"6th January, 1661-2. — This evening, according to custome, His Majesty opened the revells (at Lincoln's Inn) of that night, by throwing the dice himself in the privy chamber, where was a table set on purpose, and lost his £100 (the year before he won £1,500). The ladies also plaid very deepe.... Sorry I am that such a wretched custome as play to that excess should be countenanced in a Court that ought to be an example of virtue to the rest of the Kingdom."

During the troubled reign of James II., and during the first year of that of William III., men's minds were too harassed by political anxieties to allow them much time, or indeed inclination, to indulge in such costly and somewhat tedious entertainments. Money was scarce in England, and the few who had any, cautiously concealed even the semblance of riches, not knowing what changes a few years might produce.

Who, indeed, could predict with reasonable probability what King would rule over the land, or, indeed, which Church would gain the supremacy?

From this period these masques fell into disrepute, and the last record of so many gay revels is in 1773, on the occasion of Mr. Talbot being elevated to the woolsack.

After a long and elaborate dinner, every member of each mess had a flask of claret, besides the usual allowance of port and sack.

The Benchers then all assembled in the Great Hall, and a large ring was formed round the fireplace, when the Master of the Revels taking the Lord Chancellor by the right hand, he with his left took Mr. Justice Page, who, joined to the other Serjeants and Benchers, danced about the coal fire according to the old ceremony three times, while the ancient song, accompanied with music, was sung by one Tony Aston, dressed as a barrister.

It is difficult to understand so dignified a personage as the Lord High Chancellor inaugurating his accession to office by such an after-dinner dance.

Perhaps the extra flask of claret, following the usual port wine and sack, may have had something to do with so singular a proceeding.

At any rate, after this remarkable festival, all such hilarious proceedings ceased, and henceforward the great dinners were given with all befitting and solemn dignity.

If the grand old Hall may be deemed the heart of Gray's Inn, then the jewelled crown that is the noblest ornament of this time-honoured abode of learning may be said to have been created by the distinguished men who have grown up under her fostering care, whose studies have been matured within the shelter of her old walls.

Names are inscribed here—on the panels, on the windows, in the hall—the very sight of which must fire the heart of many a student with pride and hope.

However poor he may be, however lowly his birth, however destitute he may be of everything, save of the divine spark of genius and of that safest attendant upon genius—resolute perseverance—the path of success is open to him.

The Temple of Fame is before him. He may seize the prize it contains, if he will; but the road is steep and hard to climb, and the thorns that beset it are many and sharp.

What stories might be told of the early struggles, of the early hardships of many of those who have ultimately attained the highest places in the State and in the Law!

How many of those whose names will never die while England has a history, might relate how keen, nay, how terrible had been their sufferings when they first started in their career.

With what difficulty they obtained even necessary clothing. How hard it was to earn the daily bread. How many sacrifices had to be made, how many privations endured, ere the books could be bought that were absolutely essential for their legal studies.

And if it is thus hard for those who win, what tales of bitter woe and anguish might be written of those who labour and fail. Of those who, having both talent and application, yet lack, alas! the peculiar genius that enables the great lawyer to grasp a subject or legal point with a rapidity, and a perspicuity that is truly marvellous to the unlearned!

What hours of anxious study, what fevered days and terrible nights must the unsuccessful, struggling man endure. Conscious, in all probability, of his own deficiencies, and yet hoping on—ever hoping on, not daring to confess even to himself that the studies of years have been of no avail, that the tree is barren, and will never bear fruit.

These are the unhappy men who eventually sink into the crowd of poor legal hacks. These are indeed the jackals who must cater and work for the lions of their order.

*   *   *   *   *

NOTE.—Those who are interested in the history and customs of this old Inn of Court are referred to an admirable work on the subject, namely, "Notes on Gray's Inn," by W. R. Douthwaite, Esq., librarian.

THE TWO BROTHERS, ANTHONY AND FRANCIS BACON.

The most notable of the many distinguished names recorded in Gray's Inn is that of Francis Bacon, afterwards Lord Verulam, Viscount St. Albans, and Lord High Chancellor of England.

The son of a distinguished and learned gentleman, he was also happy in having in his mother a woman alike remarkable for her piety, her domestic virtues, and her great learning. Accomplished in no common degree in the charming arts of music and painting, few scholars of the day excelled Lady Bacon in intimate knowledge of Latin and Greek.

Francis, her second son, was born in 1561, and so early gave tokens of such exceptional talent that when very young he was honoured by the notice of Queen Elizabeth. Whatever the faults, errors, and meannesses of Queen Elizabeth as a woman, in her character of sovereign, in one respect at least, she showed herself to be well worthy to wear a crown, well worthy to govern a great people, inasmuch as she possessed to a rare extent that inestimable quality in those who have to rule, the power of appreciating genius.

Under no reign has learning been more fostered, under no reign have talented men so clustered round the throne, as during the reign of this maiden Queen.

Elizabeth appreciated the powers of, and knew when she had a distinguished statesman, and though she might ill-treat him, show herself most niggardly towards him, not unfrequently betraying cruel ingratitude, yet she ever respected his talents and caused them to be respected by others.

Both Francis Bacon and his elder brother Anthony were educated at Trinity College, Cambridge.

Anthony was a man of good and even brilliant parts, but being the eldest son of Sir Nicholas Bacon, who, besides a great legal position, had large landed estates in several of the midland counties, young Anthony was not destined to any profession. He spent much of his time in travelling, and thus became personally acquainted with most of the learned persons of the age.

In 1579, being then twenty-one, to the annoyance of his family he resolved to reside entirely in Paris, and there he remained for some years. He then went to Bourges and Geneva, and, at the latter place, lodged in the house of the celebrated Theodore Beza.

From Geneva he successively removed to Montpellier, Marseilles, Bordeaux, and Montauban, having become by this time a sort of recognised Government correspondent, constantly communicating to the English ministry intelligence of any importance.

In 1585 he went to Bearn on a visit to Henry of Navarre, afterwards the great Henry IV. of France, and here made acquaintance with the learned Lambert Dansens, who, as a mark of esteem, dedicated several of his works to his English friend.

Here, too, began for poor Sir Anthony the great romance of his life. It was at this Court that he became acquainted with a beautiful French lady, whose many charms and winning graces broke the poor baronet's heart. With some rare and gifted natures love is an integral part of life. When it is clear that love must die, life in a great measure dies too, and so it was with Sir Anthony Bacon.

His love was unsuccessful; so, sore-hearted and with broken health he left the scene of his brief happiness and of his enduring grief, and returned to England, never again to leave it. He took up his residence at Essex House, and after a time rallied sufficiently from his disappointment to resume his correspondence with some of his foreign friends. Amongst these his most constant and valued correspondent was King Henry IV. of France; but the sorrowful love romance had destroyed the most brilliant portion of his existence, and Sir Anthony never quite recovered from the pain he had then suffered.

His more celebrated brother was framed in harder mould. Before Francis was seventeen he had not only traversed the whole circle of the liberal arts as then taught, but he had begun to perceive how fallacious was the recognised philosophy of the day. And these fallacies he subsequently effectually exposed.

When the time came for leaving Cambridge, his father sent him first to France, and afterwards allowed him to make, what was called, the grand tour.

So well did he profit by his travels, that he wrote a general view of the state of Europe before he was nineteen.

He had intended carrying his researches still farther abroad, projecting a journey to Egypt and India, but the death of his father obliging him to return to England, he applied himself to the study of Common Law at Gray's Inn.

Even in these early days, the lucidity of his reasoning, the keenness of his intellect attracted the notice of many leading men.

The Earl of Essex in particular, who was a great discerner of merit, became his intimate friend, and endeavoured, though unsuccessfully, to procure for Bacon the office of Queen's Solicitor.

Failing in this, Lord Essex, to console his *protégé* under such a disappointment, generously conferred on him a present of land to the value of £1,800.

Notwithstanding, however, the friendship of so powerful a patron, and notwithstanding the favour with which the Queen already regarded him, young Francis had, during the earlier years of his career, many obstacles to contend against.

Talents so remarkable, such great patronage, and especially the favour of the monarch, created a host of enemies, all of whom decried the young aspirant with the spiteful bitterness and venom of envy. They represented him as an essentially unpractical enthusiast, whose head was filled with philosophical and speculative ideas. As one far more likely therefore to perplex, than to forward public business.

So many cabals resulted in his being unable to obtain for a considerable period either office or preferment, and he was over forty years of age before Lord Burleigh, who was then Lord Treasurer, bestowed upon him the place of Registrar to the Star Chamber.

This appointment was worth about £1,600, but its duties were both onerous and unpleasant. It so happened that to Bacon they became especially distasteful, for the critical moment arrived when he had to decide whether he would resign his preferment, or disregard every sacred claim of honour and friendship.

Unhappily the choice he made at this juncture has tarnished for ever a name, that in other respects he rendered so illustrious, and ultimately it, in fact, proved the ruin of this great and gifted man.

Even in the events of this world, how often do our own faults become the very lashes that scourge us. How frequently does the evil we have done to others return upon us fourfold.

"Cast thy bread upon the waters," says the preacher, "and after many days it shall come back to thee," and this applies to evil as well as to good deeds.

During the larger part of Queen Elizabeth's reign, both in Court and State, two great parties were for ever struggling to obtain supremacy.

The two Cecils were at the head of one of these parties.

The leader of the other was first the Earl of Leicester, and subsequently, his son-in-law, the Earl of Essex.

Bacon's undoubted genius excited both the jealousy and the dislike of his relatives, the Cecils, and the intimate friendship he had formed with Lord Essex also much increased their covert animosity, although they did not care to exhibit it openly against so near a connection.

Still, though outwardly courteous, Bacon was well aware that in them he had formidable enemies, and he knew that his future prosperity mainly depended upon his being able to convert these enemies into friends.

Essex, with the generosity that was his distinguishing characteristic, had not only exerted himself strenuously on his friend's behalf, but had also, as already mentioned, by a noble gift, sought to console him for his disappointment in failing to obtain place.

But after years of prosperity and power, the fatal day came when the favourite was to share the fate of most Royal favourites, Essex was disgraced and fell into deep misfortune.

That a man could write as Bacon afterwards wrote of "Friendship," and of "Honour and Reputation," and yet permit himself, at the base dictates of ambition, to desert, nay, even to betray his earliest and most generous friend, must seem to every noble heart a fact almost incredible; but it is unhappily an undoubted fact, that when Essex was at the bar of the House of Lords to be tried for his life. Bacon, in his professional capacity, appeared *against* his generous and affectionate friend and patron.

Nor was even this the extent of his unworthy treason.

For some time previously, and also after the unhappy favourite had expiated his follies by a shameful death, discontent and irritation had been spreading amongst all classes, and the Government grew daily more and more unpopular.

At length the clamours of the people became so loud and deep, not only against ministers, but also against the Queen herself, that it was deemed necessary to make a formal vindication of the proceedings of the Administration.

For this end all the blame, all the obloquy of every administrative failure must be thrown upon the dead man.

Bacon accepted the discreditable, nay, disgraceful duty that had been assigned to him. He allowed himself to vilify the name of his benefactor, his early friend. He agreed to cast the odium of treason upon one from whom he had accepted gifts, and for whom he had professed, and professed for years, the most ardent friendship.

In a skilful and masterly paper he justified the proceedings of the Government, and drew up a declaration of the treason of which Essex had been found guilty, and for which he had duly suffered.

Bacon retained his place. He had assured his career. He had forced the world to recognise his transcendent abilities; but ambition must have indeed hardened the heart of this man, ere she could console him for having thus cast from him every sentiment of gratitude, and affection, for having thus forsworn the honourable fealty that he owed to his benefactor and his friend.

From this moment, however, Bacon rose steadily, and, after the accession of James I., having published a brilliant pamphlet in favour of uniting the two kingdoms of England and Scotland, he rapidly obtained considerable honour.

In 1616 he was sworn of the Privy Council. He then devoted himself to reducing, and, in fact, recomposing the laws of England.

When Attorney-General he distinguished himself by his endeavours to restrain duelling, a practice at that time very frequent and very fatal.

In 1617 he was appointed Lord Keeper of the Great Seal, and the following year he was raised to the woolsack, and created Lord Verulam.

In the midst of these honours, and notwithstanding, also, the press of business, he did not forget his studies in philosophy, but in 1620 he published his great work, "Novum Organum." In 1621 he was advanced to the dignity of Viscount, and as Lord St. Albans he appeared with great splendour at the opening of Parliament.

But he had now arrived at the culminating point of his triumphs, and at the very moment when his power seemed greatest and his position most stable, his fall was near.

A very few months after Parliament had assembled, a committee of the House of Commons was appointed to inquire into the abuses that existed in the Courts of Justice; and, ere many sittings had taken place, the Chancellor was openly accused of corrupt practices.

The King, ever pusillanimous, and shrinking from giving support to a falling man, sent for Bacon, and, it is said, positively enjoined him to submit to his peers, promising to reward him afterwards!

The Chancellor, although he could have had but little faith in such promises, and foresaw his approaching ruin if he did not plead for himself, resolved, however, to obey the Royal command.

He was silent therefore under the accusations brought against him, and on the 3rd May, 1621, the House of Lords gave judgment against him, pronouncing upon him the following severe sentence:

"That he was to pay a fine of £40,000, and be confined a prisoner in the Tower, during the King's pleasure. That he should for ever be incapable of holding any place, office, or employment in the State, and that he should never again sit in Parliament, nor come within the verge of the Court."

At this distance of time the world judges him more leniently than he was then judged by his peers.

Greed of money had never been one of Bacon's failings. He loved power, place, and the good things that money can procure. He also loved his ease, and the affection and good-will of those about him; but of the gold itself he took little or no heed.

It was, in fact, to this carelessness, and to an amiability that he carried to the extent of selfish weakness that he owed his fall. For years all that he possessed had been at the service of those about him, and unhappily he was surrounded by, and had bestowed his kindness on persons, who were not only unworthy of it, but who had basely abused the confidence he had reposed in them.

We are told by Rushworth, that the Chancellor (Bacon) treasured up nothing for himself or his family, but that he was so over-indulgent to his servants, that this indulgence reached the point of conniving at their evil doings. Both his servants and his dependents were therefore profuse and extravagant, and had at their command whatever he was master of.

Too late did Bacon perceive his error. It is related that, one day during his trial, he passed through a room where several of his servants were sitting. They rose up respectfully to salute him as he went by, but said the Chancellor, "Sit down, my masters, for your rise has been my fall."

There seems little reason now to doubt that the gifts the Chancellor was accused of taking had been enforced, and received by these underlings.

It was these lamentable gifts that had caused him to be suspected of injustice, and yet it was subsequently proved that his decrees had been made for the most part with so much equity, that not one of them was ever reversed as unjust.

"It was peculiar to this man," says one of his numerous biographers, "to have nothing narrow or selfish in his composition. He gave away without concern whatever he possessed, and believing other men to be of the same mould, he received with as little consideration."

This opinion is probably correct in the main, but the greatest admirers of this talented and in many respects exceptionally great man, must admit that, ere he could have become unmindful of the honourable fealty he owed to his dead friend, the greed of power must have been strong in his heart, and that it was a selfish reluctance to take trouble that made him disregard one of the most stringent duties of the great, not only to be just themselves, but to ascertain that injustice is not practised by their subordinates.

After a short period of imprisonment the fallen Chancellor was released from the Tower. The King ultimately remitted his fine; and, after the death of James, he was again summoned to attend Parliament in the first year of the reign of Charles I., but never again after his degradation did Bacon take part in active life.

At first, indeed, after his release from prison, he found himself in extreme poverty. All he valued in this world had gone from him. Place, position, money, and, above all, that consideration from others which had been so dear to his heart.

So great at one time was his pecuniary distress, that he wrote a pathetic letter to King James, entreating His Majesty's assistance. "Lest," as he expresses it, "he should be reduced to carry a wallet, and after having lived only to study, be forced to study to live."

Notwithstanding the sorrowfulness of the letter, there lurks within it a vein of the humour that rendered him so delightful a companion, and through it all can be perceived the indomitable spirit of the man, that, even in the bitterest moment of his shattered fortunes, rose superior to the ruin that had overtaken him.

The energy that had made him so powerful in his public career did not desert him in his retirement.

With all the ardour of his great heart, he loved his country home, his quiet lodgings in Gray's Inn, and the studies to which, during the last years of his life, he wholly devoted himself. It was at this period that he wrote some of his most important English and Latin works; and from these it is evident that his thoughts were as free, and as vigorous, as they had ever been during the earliest and most brilliant years of his career.

Although he had been unhappy in having had many false and unworthy friends, one, at least, loved him faithfully to the end; and it was by him, Sir Thomas Meanty, his secretary, that the monument was erected to his memory in St. Michael's Church, St. Albans.

Many have written the biography of this distinguished man, but the best evidences of his life are the works he has given to the world: works replete with noble thoughts; works so grand, that they make us the more regret that there should be even one flaw to tarnish the golden lustre that shines around the name of one so brilliant, so illustrious.

It was in chambers in Coney Court, now called Gray's Inn Square, that Bacon passed his last years, and where he wrote several of his greatest works.

The aspect of these old houses—indeed, of these old chambers—bears traces, not only of the storms and sunshine that have passed over them in all this lapse of time, but they also speak to us powerfully of the vicissitudes of human life, and of the changes that are taking place around us yearly, nay, hourly.

What anxiety and distress, what joy and what pain, have not these old walls witnessed.

How many hearts have beat high with hope, or have been racked with anguish in the thoughtful gloom of many of these shadowy rooms.

Bacon himself, though he bore so brave a front before the world, must have had many torturing recollections and regrets as he paced up and down these ancient chambers. But then, again, what noble thoughts came to cheer and support him as he overcame the keenness of his pain, and fixed his mind on objects higher and grander than the passing events of human life.

Thus generation after generation pass away, with all their joys and all their fears.

Each human being departs, and his name is no more known even in the spot where he dwelt; but still the great squadrons of mankind are ever advancing, with the same delights, the same anxieties as those who have left this earth many hundreds of years ago; thus every place is filled and emptied, and filled again in endless rotation.

Truly life is but a magic-lantern, and the players therein are but fleeting shadows.

Bacon died on Easter Sunday, the 9th of April, 1626, being then sixty-six years of age.

In the December previous he had with his own hand written his will. In it he writes:

"For my burial, I desire it may be in St. Michael's Church near St. Albans. There was my mother buried, and it is the parish church of my mansion house at Gorhambury, and it is the only Christian church within the walls of Old Verulam. For my name and memory, I leave it to men's charitable speeches, and to foreign nations, and to the next ages."

SIR NICHOLAS BACON.

Sir Nicholas Bacon, Lord Keeper of the Great Seal during the greater part of the reign of Queen Elizabeth, was born at Chislehurst, in Kent, in 1510.

Few men have enjoyed during a long and brilliant career a more unblemished reputation for probity, or have conducted themselves in troubled and dangerous times with more prudence and good discretion than this celebrated statesman and judge.

He received his first rudiments of learning at home, and at a small village school in the neighbourhood of his father's house; but when still very young he was sent to Corpus Christi College, Cambridge.

Here he made great progress in all branches of useful knowledge, and then travelled over France, making some stay in Paris, in order, as an old chronicler remarks, "to give the last polish to his education."

Either this last polish or his natural gifts enabled him to turn his speeches with singular aptitude and felicity. Though resolute in proposing and carrying out any measure he deemed advisable, he spoke with so much prudence and tact, that he ever succeeded in retaining the good will even of his opponents.

This is all the more remarkable, for never, perhaps, did party feeling run so high, never was party animosity more bitter, both with regard to politics and also on religious subjects, than during this period, when England was convulsed by the tremendous changes that were taking place in the Church, and by the savage persecutions that had been endured and inflicted both by Protestants and by Roman Catholics.

Alas! that men, while calling themselves Christians, should so distort and make of none effect the first principles of our Divine Teacher!

When Bacon returned from Paris he settled in Gray's Inn, and applied himself with such assiduity to the study of the law, that he speedily became of note amongst the learned in that profession. His profound knowledge of many difficult points of law enabled him to be useful not only to the Government but also to the King (Henry VIII.), insomuch that, on the dissolution of the Monastery of Bury St. Edmund's, in Suffolk, King Henry conferred upon him several manors in that county.

Two years afterwards he was promoted to the office of Attorney of Wards, an appointment of both honour and profit.

Edward VI. confirmed him in this post, and in the last year of that King's reign

Bacon was elected treasurer of Gray's Inn.

His great moderation and his consummate prudence preserved him safely during the dangerous reign of Queen Mary, although he was well known to be a staunch Protestant.

No sooner did Elizabeth come to the throne, however, than he was knighted, and the Great Seals of England having been taken from Nicholas Heath, Archbishop of York, they were delivered to Sir Nicholas Bacon in November, 1558, with the title of Lord Keeper.

It is much to the credit of Sir Nicholas that he himself introduced a Bill into Parliament for the purpose of defining and settling the position of Lord Keeper; although, had he chosen to be silent, and to procure for himself the additional title of Lord Chancellor, he might have obtained almost unlimited power.

But his motto was, and ever had been, "*Mediocra firma.*" He was content to be safe, and did not desire greatness.

Unlike many celebrated men, he was unaffectedly modest, and devoid of self-seeking, so that while it was said of some other great personages that they seemed wiser than they were, the common voice of the nation agreed in this, that Sir Nicholas Bacon was even wiser than he seemed.

To the Queen he was indeed a most valuable minister, and a most trusty counsellor, for not only was he as a statesman remarkable for a clear head, and wise, farseeing sagacity, but he had marvellous skill in balancing factions, and it was thought he taught the Queen this same secret, the more important to Elizabeth, for being, as Her Majesty was, the last of her family, she was without those supports that are ordinarily incidental to Princes.

In Chancery, also, Bacon much distinguished himself by the very moderate use he made of power, and by the great respect he ever showed for the Common Law. But better than all, in an age of bigotry, when religious differences aroused in men every violent and cruel passion, Bacon showed that though his own religious opinions were strong, he could speak and act on that, as on all other subjects, with moderation and with strict equity.

The main business of the session of January, 1559, was the settlement of religious observances, and no man had a greater share in this momentous and difficult question than the Lord Keeper.

The speeches he made at this period are described by many contemporary writers as "most eloquent, solid, and excellent speeches;" and at this day we can perceive that they were, as another old chronicler observes, "models of eloquence, profound wisdom, and conciliatory discretion."

Few men have left behind them so delightful a character as this famous statesman and lawyer.

Powerful and wise in public life, in his home he was the tender father, the affectionate relative, the indulgent and unostentatious friend.

Though endowed with a keen appreciation of art, and gifted with a fine and graceful taste, as appeared by his house and gardens at Gorhambury, yet he never permitted himself to indulge in an undue or lavish expenditure. So simple and modest was he in this respect, that, when the Queen came to visit him at Redgrave, Her Majesty said she found the house too small for so great a man.

"Nay, madam," said the Chancellor, "but it is your Majesty who has made me too great for my house."

Yet, with his usual graceful tact and ready acquiescence in the wishes of his Royal Mistress, he immediately built two small wings to his house.

His health began to fail during the later years of his life, and he became distressingly corpulent; but he was as diligent in his work, and his temper remained as kind, and his wit as bright as ever.

After having held the Great Seal more than twenty years, this able statesman and faithful counsellor was suddenly removed from this life by the following accident:

He was under the hands of his barber, and the weather being rather sultry, although February, Sir Nicholas, who suffered much from heat by reason of his great size, caused the window before him to be opened. He presently fell asleep, but after a time, a current of cold air blowing upon him, he awoke shivering and feeling very ill.

"Why," said he to his servant, "did you suffer me to sleep thus exposed?"

The man replied that he durst not venture to disturb him.

"Then," said the Lord Keeper, "by your civility I lose my life." And so indeed it proved. He was removed immediately to his bed-chamber, and was tended with loving care, but he expired a very few days after being taken ill.

Sir Nicholas was twice married. By his first wife, Jane, daughter of William Fernley, he had three sons, who died young, and three daughters.

By his second wife, Anne, daughter of Sir Anthony Cooke, a woman distinguished alike for her beauty, her piety, and her learning, he had two sons, of whom the youngest, Francis, became so celebrated as Chancellor, philosopher, and writer; a man whose exceptionally brilliant gifts have thrown comparatively into the shade the far more elevated character of his father.

Happy would it have been for the son, if, with his father's talents, he had inherited his father's unswerving integrity and noble sense of honour.

Far happier would have been the closing years of Lord Bacon's life had he, like his father, Sir Nicholas, dealt righteously with all men.

SIR WILLIAM GASCOIGNE.

It is not unusual to find amongst ancient families that the same Christian name is retained from generation to generation, constantly descending for centuries in unbroken succession.

Sometimes this name is preserved in memory of a distinguished ancestor. Sometimes from respect to some prince or powerful patron who had conferred honour or lands upon the family.

Many have supposed that the name of William came to this country at the time of the Norman Conquest. It has been ascertained, however, that long before that date it was in common use in Saxon families, especially amongst those who inhabited the Northern Counties.

This name William is a German word, and, according to Martin Luther, of compound meaning.

Helm, signifying "defence;" and *Kenhelm*, "Defence of kindred."

Willy, *Villi*, or *Billi* with the Germans, like *Poly* amongst the Greeks, before several names indicates "many," consequently *Wilhelm*, now softened into *William*, means "Much defence" or "Defence of many."

Not only did the Normans, who had settled here when their Duke became King of England, call their sons after their victorious sovereign, but many of the old lords of the soil, who, wearied with Harold's tyranny, had gladly welcomed the advent of the foreign prince, gave their children the name now so much in vogue. In addition to this compliment to their new King, some of the Saxon Thanes and great landed proprietors moulded their rougher Northern surnames into courtly Norman terminations.

Thus Gaskin, an old West Riding family, Normanised itself into Gascoigne.

As time went on, this Royal name of William was regularly transmitted from father to son amongst those families who depended upon the Conqueror or his line, or who had received gifts of offices, lands, seignories, or privileges, until in a few years it became so common amongst those of high rank, that at a certain festival given at the Court of King Henry II., when Sir William St. John and Sir William Fitz-Hamon, two especial officers, commanded that none "but those of the name of William should dine in the Great Chamber with them," they were accompanied by a hundred and twenty Williams, all knights.

Sir William Gascoigne, Chief Justice of the King's Bench in 1401, the second year of the reign of King Henry IV., was the eighth Sir William in lineal descent, and was succeeded, as we learn from Dugdale and Fuller, by seven more Sir Williams, all knights.

The Chief Justice was born in 1350, *temp.* Edward III., at Gawthorp, in the parish of Harwood, between Leeds and Knaresborough.

Sir William was the eldest of five brothers. He married twice: first, Elizabeth, daughter and heiress of Alexander Mowbray, and by her had an only son, Sir William Gascoigne, of Gawthorp, a brave commander in the wars under King Henry V. His descendant, the last Sir William of this branch, married Beatrice, daughter of Sir Richard Tempest, and had four sons, all of whom died young, and one daughter, Margaret, his sole heir, in whom the Gascoignes of this line terminated. This daughter married, in 1552, Thomas Wentworth, of Wentworth Woodhouse, in Yorkshire, and brought great estates into that family. Thomas Wentworth was Sheriff for Yorkshire in the twenty-fourth year of Queen Elizabeth, and had, besides four daughters, an only son, who became afterwards Sir William Wentworth, and was the father of Thomas, first Earl of Strafford.

The Chief Justice married, secondly, Joan, daughter of Sir William Pickering, and widow of Sir Ralph Graystock, Baron of the Exchequer. By this marriage Sir William had also an only son, James Gascoigne, settled at Cardington, in Bedfordshire. A descendant of this James Gascoigne, the inheritrix of Cardington, married her distant cousin William, a younger son of the Gascoignes of Gawthorp.

This William Gascoigne was Sheriff for Bedfordshire in 1506, *temp.* King Henry VII., and was Sheriff for Buckinghamshire in the fifth year of King Henry VIII. He was subsequently knighted by Henry VIII., and became Comptroller of the Household to Cardinal Wolsey; for the great Cardinal in many respects affected Royal state, and succeeded in having the chief offices of his household held by nobles, or by men of gentle birth. This branch of the Gascoignes also terminated in a daughter, Dorothy, who married Sir Jarrett Harvye; thus the direct descendants of the famous Chief Justice became merged in other families. Of collateral descendants, however, there are many; Nicholas Gascoigne of Lavingcroft, Sir William's next brother, having left a numerous family of sons and daughters, who married amongst the Percys, Latimers, Vavasours, etc.

From the eldest son of this Nicholas descended a somewhat celebrated man, Richard Gascoigne, who was not only a learned antiquary and collector, but who has done good service to the history of this country by having brought before the public in 1638 Mr. Dugdale, whose writings have given much interesting and important information.

The greater part of the valuable collections made by Richard Gascoigne is now at Wentworth Woodhouse, Yorkshire. There are also relics of the Gascoigne family at Ickwellbury, Bedfordshire.

William Gascoigne became a student of the Law at Gray's Inn, and was early enrolled a member of that learned Society. His career was both brilliant and rapid. Towards the end of the reign of King Richard II. he was already so eminent in his profession that, in 1398, he was made one of the King's Serjeants.

There are records of many transactions at this period, all of which give proof, not only of Gascoigne's great abilities as a lawyer, but also testify to the esteem in which he was held on account of the fidelity and uprightness of his advice, and the invariable justice of his decisions. His great merits caused him to be appointed one of the Commissioners for Henry of Lancaster, Duke of Hereford, when this Prince was about to go into banishment.

Gascoigne had to watch over the interests and receive all moneys that might come to the Duke during his absence from England. A most onerous appointment, involving not only considerable difficulty but also no inconsiderable danger, for in those turbulent days the law of might frequently warred most successfully against the law of right.

So early as the second year of the reign of King Henry IV., Gascoigne was made Chief Justice of the King's Bench, and we find that in 1403 Judge Gascoigne and Ralph Nevill, Earl of Westmoreland, were commissioned by the King to levy and assemble forces in the counties of York and Northumberland in order to quell the insurrection of Henry Percy, Earl of Northumberland.

Somewhat later these Commissioners were also empowered to treat with this same rebellious Earl.

When Archbishop Scrope and others were taken in arms against the King, His Majesty would have had Gascoigne immediately to give sentence of death against the contumacious Archbishop; but the Chief Justice refused, resolutely declaring he would not pronounce such a sentence in so irregular and illegal a manner. This refusal brought upon him the King's high displeasure, but the people praised him much for his justice and his moderation.

Again, when certain abbots, priors, knights, esquires, and other persons of distinction had been wrongfully accused, and were suffering imprisonment in consequence of the evidence of a perjured witness, Sir William detected the fraud. He then caused the false witness to be exposed and condemned, and obtained the release of the guiltless persons.

About this time, also, attorneys, by reason of their multitude, and from their malpractices, had grown to be a public nuisance. Chief Justice Gascoigne caused an Act to be passed limiting their number in every county. They had also to swear every Term that they would deal faithfully and truly by their clients, and could it be proved that they had not done so they were liable to be imprisoned for a twelve-month and condemned to pay a ransom according to the King's pleasure.

In the abstract of the Parliament rolls there is a lone insertion made of a curious and important case referred in part to the judgment of the Chief Justice. William, Lord Roos of Hamalake, brought an action against Sir Robert Therwit, one of the Justices of the King's Bench, inasmuch as he had withheld certain manors and commons in the county of Lincoln, and that he had lain in wait with five hundred men to seize or apprehend the said Lord. Sir Robert confessed his fault before the King, and offered to abide by the award of two Lords of the complainant's kindred.

These two Lords made a long judgment, and amongst other items enjoined that Sir Robert should make a great feast at Milton-le-Roos. That for this feast he should prepare two fat oxen, twelve sheep, two tuns of Gascon wine, and other provisions. That he should then assemble there all such knights, esquires, and yeomen as had been his accomplices. That they should then confess their fault to Lord Roos, craving his pardon, and offering him five hundred marks as compensation. Lord Roos should refuse this sum, but he should pardon them, and partake of their dinner.

The arbitration respecting the land however, which was the point of the greatest difficulty, was to be referred to Sir William Gascoigne, the Chief Justice.

But the event which became so noticeable in legal and in historical annals, is a remarkable circumstance that has been described by many writers, namely, his having committed the Heir Apparent to the Throne, Prince Henry, to prison for contempt of Court.

A story so extraordinary has of course been seized upon by dramatists and poets, who have so embellished the original history, that they have caused the fact to be doubted by some. However, the affair has been too simply related by some of our best historians and other grave writers to permit reasonable doubts that the circumstance did actually take place as recorded.

It appears that a servant of Prince Henry's being arraigned at Westminster before Chief Justice Gascoigne for felony, the Prince, hearing of the matter, came hastily into Court, and commanded that his follower should be unfettered and set at liberty immediately.

This demand was refused, the Chief Justice exhorting the Prince to be patient, for his servant was to be tried according to the ancient laws of the realm, adding that even in case the rigour of the law should condemn the accused, His Highness might still obtain the gracious pardon of the King, his father.

Far from being appeased by this answer, the anger of the Prince seemed only the more inflamed, and striding fiercely to the Bar, he endeavoured to rescue the prisoner by force.

Thereupon the Judge, with admirable courage and intrepidity, commanded the Prince to forbear and to depart on his way; but the Prince's rage at being thus thwarted made him quite beside himself, and, turning hastily towards the Bench, he either struck, or endeavoured to strike, the Chief Justice.

At so unparalleled an insult the Court was stricken with horror, and many threw themselves around the Judge, fearing the Prince was about to slay him, but Sir William, nothing moved by the affront that had been offered to him, nor by the peril in which he was placed, never stirred from his seat, and with dignified calm, and with a bold and assured countenance, said to the Prince:

"Sir, remember yourself. I keep here the place of your Sovereign Lord and father, to whom you owe double obedience. Wherefore in his name I charge you, desist from your wilfulness, and from this unlawful enterprise. From henceforth give good example to them, who hereafter will be your own subjects. And now, for your contempt and disobedience, go you to the prison of the King's Bench, whereunto I commit you, and remain there a prisoner, until the pleasure of the King your father be further known."

So dignified was the Judge's bearing, so noble and calm were his few coercive sentences, wherein were combined the paternal authority of the King, and the awful gravity of the Judge, that the Prince was instantly subdued.

His Highness at once laid aside his weapon, and doing reverence to the Court, he straightway withdrew, and submitted to the disgraceful punishment—a punishment degrading indeed to a Prince, the Heir Apparent to the Throne, but well merited from the outrageous insult that had led to it.

When some officious persons represented the affair to the King in such a manner that His Majesty might well have taken offence at it, the wise monarch, the wise father, defeated the ill-will of the informers by "thanking God, who had given him not only a judge who could minister, but also a son who could obey justice."

Prince Henry had been carefully educated and governed at the University of Oxford, and was afterwards for some years engaged with his father's armies in stilling the commotions constantly taking place on the borders of Wales. He seems to have done well also when first appointed President of the Council, for again our old chronicler tells us that the Commons voted him thanks for his good employment of the treasure; but, unhappily, before his Royal father's death he abandoned himself to dissolute courses, and made discreditable associates his intimate companions and friends.

After his father's death, however, on ascending the throne as Henry V., he discarded his unworthy followers, and applied himself with both assiduity and talent to the government of his kingdom.

We learn from Tressel's continuation of "Daniel's Collection of the History of England, 1641," that the King, addressing himself to his former friends, said:

"It was sufficient that for many years he had fashioned himself according to their unruly dispositions, and had wandered with them in a wilderness of riot and unthriftiness; whereby he had made himself almost an alien to the hearts of his father and allies, and had so disparaged himself, that in the eyes of mankind his presence was grown vulgar and stale, and like the cuckoo in June, was heard but not regarded." The King then proceeds to relate in brief, that when one of his associates was summoned before the Lord Chief Justice he had interposed, and had even struck the Judge, and that for this offence he had deservedly been committed to prison by the Chief Justice. The King thus terminates his speech: "For which act of justice I shall ever hold him worthy of the place and of my favour. I wish all my judges to have the like undaunted courage to punish offenders of what rank soever."

It is greatly to the honour of Henry V. that the brave and good old Chief Justice retained his post until age and infirmities compelled him to relinquish it.

Sir William Gascoigne appeared in his place in Parliament and sat in Court in Westminster Hall during the first year of the reign of King Henry V. But his long and arduous career had aged him before the allotted threescore years and ten that are given to man, and in 1413 he quitted public life.

He did not long survive his retirement, but, after a short illness, expired within a year of his resignation.

His funeral was celebrated with the magnificence due to his eminent dignity, his honourable family, his large fortune, and his exalted fame.

On a stately monument in Harwood Church, Yorkshire, where he was interred, he is represented lying at full length, attired in his judge's robes, with a hood drawn over his head. At his right side is a long dagger; on the left, a purse fastened to his girdle. One of his wives lies beside him. There are the remains of an inscription cut in brass around the edge of the tomb. Unfortunately, during the Civil Wars much of this brass-work was torn away.

In the east window of the same church there still remain some portions of the ancient glass, and in this glass can be traced the figure of a man arrayed in the scarlet robes of a judge. Both on his right hand and on his left is the figure of a kneeling woman, and above these three figures are the arms of the Gascoigne family, and also those of the Mowbrays and of the Pickerings.

LORD BURLEIGH.

William Cecil, Baron of Burleigh, Burghley, or Burley, for some time Secretary of State during the reigns of Edward VI. and Queen Elizabeth, and eventually Lord High Treasurer of England, was one of the ablest statesmen, one of the worthiest ministers that England, or indeed, any other country, has ever possessed.

He was born at Bourne, in Lincolnshire, in 1520, and was educated at the Grammar Schools of Grantham and Stamford.

He was then sent to St. John's College, Cambridge, where, finding himself associated with several young men of much talent, he was seized with such a vehement passion for learning, that it is related of him that he hired the bell-ringer to call him up every morning at four o'clock.

Unfortunately, he applied himself with too much zeal to his studies, for, by neglecting to take due precautions to keep himself in health, he brought on a severe illness, of which he was with difficulty cured.

Amongst other painful disorders, want of exercise caused his legs to swell to an immense size; and his physicians always declared that this distressing illness laid the foundation of the severe attacks of gout from which he suffered greatly during the latter years of his life.

However, during his youth, no amount of suffering could subdue his passion for learning.

He doubtless loved knowledge for the sake of acquiring knowledge; but, at the same time, it is evident from the notes he made, that a keen desire to excel all his companions and contemporaries was one of the chief spurs to his exertions.

At sixteen he read a "Lecture on Sophistry," and at nineteen he had written a lecture in Greek, a very remarkable circumstance, even amongst students at this time, as there were but few men, either at Cambridge or elsewhere, who were so perfectly masters of Greek that they could write and deliver a discourse in that language.

From Cambridge he proceeded to Gray's Inn, where he soon attracted attention, both by his energy and by the assiduity with which he applied himself to the intricate study of the law.

He was happy in the possession of two excellent qualities, qualities not often found united in the same person, sound judgment, and a remarkably retentive memory. He strengthened these powers not only by indefatigable application, but also by his habit of recording with his pen every incident or remark that appeared to him worthy of notice, both when reading or from observation. The prodigious number of notes he has left behind him, testify to the marvellous industry and care with which he devoted himself to any subject of interest.

He also seized every opportunity of meeting and conversing with clever men, delighting much in free disputes upon all sorts of subjects, by which means he early became an eloquent and a correct speaker.

He had originally intended to adopt the Law as a profession, but chance introduced him to the knowledge of, and led to his obtaining the favour of his Sovereign.

Happening one day to pay a visit to his father, who was at that time Master of the Robes to the King, he met there two priests, chaplains to O'Neill, a famous Irish Chief, who was then at the English Court. Falling into a violent dispute with them, touching the supremacy of the Pope, young Cecil displayed so much skill in the argument, which was carried on in Latin, that the circumstance came to the King's ears.

Henry, who was one of the most learned princes of the age, and who delighted in learned people, desired to see the young man who had evinced such remarkable talent, and was so favourably impressed with Cecil's good manners and good conversation, that he presently gave him the reversion of the post of *Custos brevium*.

This early introduction to Court led to an alteration of plans with respect to the Law; and as Cecil's marriage, which took place soon afterwards, with the daughter of Sir John Cheeks, brought him to the notice of the Duke of Somerset, he resolved to devote himself to the career that was now open to him.

The Protector, the Duke of Somerset, took him into great favour, and soon appointed him Master of Requests, a position of considerable importance; and in 1547 still further promoted him by advancing him to the dignity of a Secretary of State.

As another mark of regard the Protector allowed Cecil to accompany him to Scotland — a proof of affection that had well-nigh cost the young statesman his life. At the battle of Musselburgh Cecil must have been killed in the *mêlée*, had not one of his friends saved him at the expense of losing his own arm.

Within a year after the Scottish expedition the Duke of Somerset fell into disgrace, and Cecil, sharing in the misfortunes of his friend and patron, was also sent to prison, where he remained three months. On the accession of Elizabeth, however, he was not only set at liberty, but he was reinstated in his office of Secretary of State, and in 1561 the additional appointment of Master of Wards was conferred upon him.

Notwithstanding all these dignities and emoluments, his life at this time was a sorely troubled one. Not only did factious opposition distract both the Government and the Kingdom, but endless conspiracies were formed that threatened each one of the Ministry. Like the old fable of the dragon's teeth, no sooner was one plot discovered and crushed than another arose in its place.

In Leicester also Cecil had a powerful and formidable rival; but the favourite, unfortunately for himself, was intemperate in speech, and rash and violent in action.

Cecil, on the contrary, was remarkable, not only for the control he possessed over his temper during political controversies, but also for the moderation of the opinions he gave to the world. All men also agreed that he was eminently just.

The Queen, therefore, was far too clear-sighted not to perceive how valuable a minister, how judicious a counsellor she had in Cecil. The Queen also saw plainly that Cecil's interests were intimately interwoven with her own; and this wise Sovereign perfectly understood that he was fitted to be her adviser and her minister whose personal welfare, and indeed safety, depended upon the *success* of the counsels that he gave.

Thus, amidst all the political storms and tempests that convulsed these troubled times, Cecil, by his skill and prudence, steered both himself and his Royal Mistress safely through the rocks and shoals by which they were surrounded. Others rose and fell, but Cecil ever maintained his position, and year by year gained fresh honours.

In 1571 he was raised to the Peerage by the title of Baron Burleigh. He was soon afterwards appointed Lord High Treasurer, and the great distinction of the Garter was bestowed upon him.

But while his public life was thus brilliant, his heart was bowed down by domestic affliction. His first wife had lived but a few years, and after her death he married Mildred, daughter of Sir Anthony Cooke and elder sister of Anne Cooke, afterwards Lady Bacon.

These sisters were remarkable for their beauty, their accomplishments, and their learning. They were well skilled in music, could converse in many foreign tongues, and in their knowledge of Latin and Greek were equal to some of the most famous scholars of the day. Both these fair and charming women not only obtained but succeeded in keeping the strong love of their husbands.

After a married life of forty-three years, the loss of the wife he had so fondly loved rendered Lord Burleigh a broken-hearted man. His health gave way under the excess of his affliction, and, for the first time during his long and arduous career, he felt himself unable to perform the duties of his office.

He became changed in many ways. The brightness and cheerfulness of his temper left him. He grew silent and melancholy, and from the sad hour when she, who had been the angel in his house, was taken from him, he never regained that sunny hopefulness of disposition that in happier days had been one of his peculiar characteristics.

He entreated the Queen to allow him to resign, for he desired now to spend the remainder of his days in quiet and retirement; but Elizabeth, well aware that his abilities were as brilliant as ever, was unwilling to part with her most trusted counsellor.

He yielded to the Royal command, and from this time laboured if possible more assiduously than ever, giving himself neither rest nor relaxation. Notwithstanding such prodigious exertions, and the acute sufferings he endured from attacks of gout, his life was prolonged beyond the usual age of man.

His last memorable public act was endeavouring to give peace to his country, when reasonable terms might have been obtained from Spain.

These terms, though considered reasonable by Burleigh, were violently opposed by the Earl of Essex; who, having gained some reputation by the sword, was unwilling to favour peace.

He, in fact, expressed himself in such passionate language, that the Lord Treasurer, after listening for a considerable time in calm silence, was at length moved to say, "that the noble Lord seemed intent on nothing but blood and slaughter."

Then he pulled out a prayer-book, and with a dignity befitting his age and experience, and with an earnestness that deeply impressed those around, he pointed to the following words: "Men of blood shall not live out half their days." This was his last appearance in public.

Never again did Lord Burleigh attend either Council or Parliament, but even when confined to his bed during the last trying and suffering illness, he prepared and settled a new treaty between the Queen and the States, whereby this nation was relieved of an expense of one hundred and twenty thousand pounds per annum.

Then, having filled the highest and most important offices of State, in the seventy-eighth year of his age, calmly and peacefully, about five o'clock in the morning of the 4th of August, 1598, surrounded by his children and grandchildren, his dearest friends, and by many old and faithful servants, he passed away from this life, full of years, rich in honours, at peace with all men, and humbly trusting by the mercy of his God, he should again see her whom he had so passionately loved.

The history of Burleigh's life is the history of England during one of the most anxious and troubled, but also one of the most memorable and glorious periods this country has ever known.

For forty years this great statesman guided the helm of Government, and although the Queen from time to time allowed others to have influence with her, yet whenever difficulties arose or matters occurred of more than ordinary moment, it was in her long-tried and faithful Minister that Elizabeth invariably confided.

The moderate views, the calm foresight and wisdom of this consummate politician, caused him not only to be regretted after his death, but to be valued during his life, a good fortune that but rarely falls to the lot of even the most celebrated political leaders.

Burleigh deserved, and he obtained, the esteem and respect both of his Sovereign and of her people, and from the beginning to the end of his glorious career, however much men may have differed from him in opinion, they ever acknowledged his honesty of purpose, his hearty love for his country, and his earnest desire to increase both her prosperity and her renown.

At this distance of time, when subsequent events have shown the fallacy of most of the hopes and fears that then influenced mankind, many may see reason to disapprove of his policy; but it must be remembered that in the sixteenth century swords were more readily drawn than they now are. Measures that to-day seem needlessly harsh, were often forced upon statesmen of that period by the fears and also suspicions of their own partisans.

Not only was Burleigh gifted with talents beyond the ordinary endowments of men, but in all outward seeming Nature had been lavish in her kindly gifts to him. Well-shaped, handsome, and graceful in person, he also possessed in no common degree that winning charm of manner that not only gains the affection of friends, but which also adds such especial happiness to the intercourse of domestic life.

His mode of living was such as became a man of high rank, entertaining with magnificent hospitality all those who, from rank, merit, and talent, were entitled to his acquaintance. To every one who came to his house he was courteous and cheerful, for he held that a host should not, by silent or reserved behaviour, mar the enjoyment of his guests.

Whenever he could obtain a little relaxation from the press of public business, he would hasten to the country, for his great delight was to improve and beautify both his family seat at Burleigh and his house and gardens at Theobalds; but above all he loved Theobalds, and, as he expresses it, always fled there whenever it was possible to bury himself in its delightful privacy.

Lord Burleigh had also two other places of residence—his lodgings at Court, and his house on the Strand. In his house in London he had fifty persons of his family, and his expenses there, he writes to a friend, were thirty pounds a week when absent, and between forty and fifty when present. At Theobalds he had thirty persons of his household. Besides the sum he gave away in charity, he directed that ten pounds a week were always to be laid out in keeping the "poor" at work in his gardens. His stables cost him about a thousand marks a year.

In his service, or, rather, in his household, he had ever young men of much distinction, they deeming it an honour to serve him.

Besides his customary hospitality, he several times entertained the Queen sumptuously, and at an expense of many thousand pounds.

He built three fine houses—one in London, on the Strand, another at Theobalds, and a third at Burleigh. All these houses were, though large and grand, still more remarkable from their neatness and general convenience.

Though thus spending both liberally and magnificently, Burleigh was ever prudent and careful. He took good heed as to how his money went. He kept rigid accounts, and attended carefully, even minutely, to all domestic matters.

Writing to a friend respecting household arrangements, he says:

"My house of Burghley is of my mother's inheritance, who liveth and is the owner thereof. I am but a farmer; yet, when I am in the country, I must buy my grain, my beef, my mutton; and, for my stable, I buy my hay for the greatest part, my oats and my straw totally."

When in the country he loved to walk about and talk to the country folk, and would often stop to soothe little children in their troubles, or watch them in their play, so gentle was his temper, so abundant was his good-nature.

At his death, notwithstanding his liberal and magnificent expenditure, and though he was so little avaricious that he made less during his forty years of office than most men at that period would have made in seven, so prudently had he managed his affairs, that he left about £4,000 a year in land, £11,000 in money, and about £14,000 in valuable effects.

SIR EDWARD COKE.

Although Sir Edward Coke, Lord Chief Justice of the King's Bench during the reign of James I., was not a member of the Ancient and Honourable Society of Gray's Inn, yet, as his portrait hangs in the Great Hall, and as he occupied himself much in the affairs of this Inn of Court, a few words respecting this eminent lawyer may not be misplaced here.

There has probably never been a more consummate master of his profession than Sir Edward Coke. His interest in it amounted to enthusiasm. He loved to grapple with every legal difficulty, and brought to bear upon all its intricate technicalities a dispassionate calmness that unfortunately failed him in the ordinary affairs of life. For this reason he was even a greater man during the periods of his disgrace than when most triumphant.

During these seasons of enforced retirement he could devote himself to a subject that he loved, and with which he was thoroughly conversant, whereas the too great energy of his character, whilst in the enjoyment of successful power, led to his giving way to intemperate violence both of expression and action.

Like most distinguished lawyers, success came to him early in life. One of his first cases was a remarkable one, and brought him much credit.

Mr. Edward Denny was Vicar of Northlinham in Norfolk, and the then Lord Cromwell, who lived in the neighbourhood, procured two persons to preach several sermons in Mr. Denny's church.

Both these persons took the opportunity thus afforded them of inveighing against the Book of Common Prayer, styling it superstitious and impious.

For this reason, the Vicar, having learnt they had no license, when one of them came next to preach would have prevented him, but the man being protected by Lord Cromwell insisted on preaching, and did preach.

This proceeding caused warm words to pass between Lord Cromwell and the Vicar, the former saying:

"Thou art a false varlet, and I like not of thee."

To which the latter replied:

"It is no marvel that you like not of me, as you like those others" (meaning the preachers) "that maintain sedition against the Queen's proceedings."

Upon this Lord Cromwell brought an action against the Vicar, *de scandalis magnatum*. The defendant justified, thereupon the plaintiff demurred, and the bar was held insufficient; but upon a motion in arrest of judgment, that the declaration was insufficient, the Court gave judgment for the defendant.

Lord Cromwell then brought another action, and so the matter went on for years until Coke became engaged in the case, and he so skilfully seized the opportunity of managing and reporting it that his name was at once brought favourably before the public.

His marriage with Bridgett, daughter and co-heiress of John Paxton, Esq., a lady, with whom he had £35,000, and who was allied to some of the most powerful families in the kingdom, doubtless aided him in his career, although in after life he was wont to boast that he had triumphed neither by "pen nor purse," signifying thereby that he had never craved any man's help, nor had he ever opened his purse to buy any place.

His perfect knowledge of the laws of England, and his wonderful memory in recalling every technical circumstance bearing on or connected with those laws, was something marvellous. For this reason his judgments on all legal points have ever been held to be of exceeding value.

Unhappily in criminal trials his warmth of temper and his violence of language tended much to injure his reputation and to lessen him in the opinion of the world. Still, in spite of these great defects, his unequalled talents forced men to yield to his judgment, and however much they might condemn him they bowed to his will.

A notable instance of this occurred during the famous trial of Sir Walter Raleigh.

Sir Edward Coke, who was then Attorney-General, conducted the case on behalf of the Crown, and expressed himself with such energy against the prisoner, that Lord Cecil at length interfered and desired him to be more patient.

Much offended, Coke at once sat down, and preserved an angry silence. At length the Commissioners were compelled to entreat him to continue his address. For some time he refused; then suddenly rising, with a power and skill that electrified all present, he recapitulated the charges. So powerful were his words, so lucid were his arguments, that it was evident from that moment that the prisoner's doom was sealed.

The scene that day in the Court at Winchester, where the trial took place, must have been alike impressive and sorrowful.

The handsome, gallant Sir Walter Raleigh, the quondam favourite of the Queen, for years the popular hero of the nation, now worn and bent by age and many troubles, is standing at the bar, to be tried for his life, accused of treason against his Sovereign and against his country.

Brave he has ever been, brave he is now, and the noble face, though pale and haggard, is stern and composed. Unmoved in look or action, he listens attentively to the words of one who is urging the Judges, with all the might of burning eloquence, to pronounce him worthy of death.

Perchance for one moment a gleam of hope may have entered the prisoner's breast when he heard Lord Cecil speak, but if so, it must have been speedily dispelled when the Attorney-General addressed the Court.

Spare in form, exquisitely neat in dress, passionate in action and emphasis, the fiery and searching eye of the great lawyer seems to scan alike the thoughts as well as the faces of those on whom he looks. And his voice, deep yet penetrating, has a ring that stirs men's hearts, and brings conviction in its very accents.

With terrible minuteness, and with crushing legal skill, he states every circumstance that can tell against the accused, and each powerfully-worded sentence that fell from the lips of the Counsel for the Crown must, to the friends of the unhappy man, have been as another nail driven into the coffin that awaited him.

Long ere that famous speech was ended, hope and suspense must have been over for the prisoner. The evidence against him had been slender, but Coke's eloquence prevailed. Sir Walter was found guilty, and condemned to death.

For a month he lay in prison, daily expecting his execution. Then he was reprieved, and sent to the Tower, where he remained a prisoner for sixteen long years.

After his release, he organised an expedition to Guiana, but, failing in this, he returned to England, where he was soon after seized, imprisoned, and beheaded, not for any fresh crime or misdemeanour, but solely on the strength of his former trial and condemnation nineteen years previously. He was executed in Old Palace Yard, 1618, and died, as he had lived, a brave and resolute man.

Coke's speech on this occasion, and also another made at the trial of Sir Everard Digby, are masterpieces of skill and intelligence; but, although such brilliant displays of eloquence and learning increased his reputation as a lawyer, or rather as an orator, it was felt by the world in general that he had permitted himself a license of expression not seemly in one who held so high and responsible a position.

These speeches, nevertheless, led to his promotion, for soon afterwards he was appointed Chief Justice of the Common Pleas.

This place fulfilled all his ambition, and here he would have willingly remained, but his bitter tongue, his caustic remarks, his intolerance of the least opposition, made him many enemies, many detractors.

His foes calculated that were he placed in a position of greater power, and therefore of greater prominence, his many faults of temper would, notwithstanding his profound legal knowledge, speedily lead to his downfall.

They suggested, therefore, that his talents merited a higher post, and after a time they succeeded in having him raised to the more elevated, but, in those days, perilous position of Chief Justice of the King's Bench, or as he styled himself, Chief Justice of England.

They calculated, and the result showed they were correct, that on account of the class of cases ordinarily brought within the jurisdiction of the King's Bench, the Chief Justice would ere long find himself at antagonism with the Court.

The annals of the Law Courts at this period of English history are terrible to read. It is frightful to see on what slight grounds men were accused, tried, convicted, and executed for treason.

Verily, in those days our laws appeared to have been written in blood; but, notwithstanding their severity, it was for having shown too great *leniency* in an affair that occurred about two years after he was made Chief Justice that Sir Edward lost the King's favour.

This extraordinary and dreadful business was the discovery that Sir Thomas Overbury had been murdered in the Tower, and as light was gradually thrown on this dark matter, it became more and more evident that great and powerful personages were deeply implicated, not only in the foul murder, but also in other crimes of the most heinous and disgraceful description.

In tracing and detecting the secrets of this black business, Lord Chief Justice Coke showed so much zeal and diligence that he succeeded in having apprehended and brought to justice some of the (apparently) principal culprits, in spite, not only of the attempts that were first made to enable them to escape, but of the influence that was afterwards employed to stay their execution.

Richard Weston, who had been Overbury's keeper in the Tower, was early brought to trial. At first he seemed resolved to be silent on every subject, induced thereto, it is said, by an immense bribe from the Earl of Somerset, but at length he was prevailed on to plead.

Poor wretch, the "persuasions" to which he yielded were the thumbscrew and the rack, but no sooner did he plead than he was speedily convicted and executed. Even at the foot of the gallows the miserable creature was not left in peace. Lord Clare, Sir John Wentworth, and Mr. Lumsden (friends of Somerset) attended him to the scaffold, and vehemently urged him to declare, in these his last moments, that a conspiracy had been concocted against Somerset.

So evident was it that Overbury's murder concealed even darker secrets, and that these secrets implicated powerful and therefore formidable personages, that Sir Edward, with his keen legal foresight, early foresaw peril. So imminent, indeed, did he consider the danger, that he went to the King at Royston to beg His Majesty would appoint a commission to assist him during the necessary investigations, and thus in some degree enable him to share the onus with others.

It has been hinted by some historians that the King knew more about this hateful matter than he cared to acknowledge.

James I. was a shrewd and prudent man; he was timid also, and ever shrank from allowing his name to be involved in any way with affairs that would be distasteful to, or unpopular amongst, his newly-acquired people. His shrewdness and his fears, however, led in several instances to his acting in both a cowardly and a treacherous manner.

In this case, whatever may have been the knowledge the King possessed, he skilfully concealed his suspicions from the chief person implicated. When informed of Overbury's murder, without a moment's delay he despatched a messenger to the Chief Justice, desiring him to arrest Lord Somerset.

Sir Edward Coke at that time lived in the Temple, and so methodically did he measure out his time, that every hour had its appointed usage. One of his rules was to go to bed at nine of the clock, and to rise at three in the morning.

The Royal messenger arrived at the Temple about 1 a.m., and at once proceeded to Sir Edward's lodging. Sir Edward's son was there, and also some friends, but the Chief Justice was in bed.

Mr. Coke therefore received the messenger, who said:

"I come, sir, from His Majesty the King, and must have instant speech with your father."

"Though you come from the King," said Mr. Coke, "you cannot and shall not see my father, for if he be disturbed in his sleep he will not be fit for any business; but if you will do as we do, you shall be welcome. In two hours my father will rise, and you can then do as you please."

To this proposal the messenger was compelled to assent, so he waited.

At three o'clock, Sir Edward rang a little bell to give notice to his servant to come to him.

The Royal messenger then entered, and gave the King's letter to the Chief Justice, who at once made out the warrant for Somerset's apprehension.

The messenger went post-haste back to Royston with the warrant, and on being introduced into the Royal presence, found the King sitting with his arm round the favourite's neck.

When the officer with the fatal document entered the room, James was saying to the man whom he himself was causing to be arrested on a charge of murder: "When shall I see thee again?" the favourite being on the eve of his departure for London.

Somerset, when arrested by Sir Edward's warrant, exclaimed indignantly at the affront thus offered to a peer of the realm, even in the presence of the King's Majesty. In his anger he appealed to James.

"Nay, man," said the King, "if Coke sends for *me*, I must go."

No sooner, however, was Somerset out of the room, than his wily master added:

"Now the de'il go with thee, man, for I will never see thy face any more."

It is difficult to understand what was really the King's belief, or what were really the King's motives, on this occasion.

To some persons he asserted that he did not believe Somerset had anything to do with the actual murder. Yet it was he who caused his favourite to be arrested; and when that arrest had been made and the Chief Justice had arrived at Royston, the King spoke with exceeding angry energy, charging Sir Edward to prosecute the affair with the utmost diligence.

He was to search into the very bottom of the conspiracy, and to spare no man, however great he might be; the King concluding his adjuration thus:

"God's curse be upon you and yours if *you* spare any of them, and God's curse be upon *me* and mine, if *I* spare any one of them."

Not only the Earl of Somerset, but his wife, the young and beautiful Countess of Somerset, was also arrested as being implicated in the crime; and whilst their trials were in course of preparation, many other persons of inferior rank were tried, condemned, and executed.

On the 7th November, Mrs. Anne Turner, who had been about Lady Somerset from her childhood, was tried, convicted, and hanged.

On the 16th of the same month, Sir George Ellways, Lieutenant of the Tower, was also convicted, and was hanged on Tower Hill on the 20th.

A week later, namely, on the 27th, James Franklin was tried, convicted, and, a few days afterwards, hanged.

It might have been supposed that so many trials and executions showed no want of zeal on the part of the Chief Justice and the other Commissioners. Yet notwithstanding so sanguinary a list, Sir Edward fell into disfavour for not hunting down and giving over to the gibbet more of these miserable victims—victims who in all probability had been but the creatures and tools of those who were far more deeply implicated, and far more deeply culpable.

It has been supposed that the friends of Somerset trusted that the nation would at length weary of so much bloodshed, and that time and political events would cause the recollection of one black crime to fade away.

At any rate, the delays which were for ever arising before Lord and Lady Somerset could be brought to trial, were mainly attributed to the unwillingness of many great personages (if not actually the Court) to have certain secret transactions disclosed.

At length, however, the trial took place, Lord Chancellor Ellesmere sitting as High Steward.

The King's instructions were produced to the Commissioners, by which they were directed to try, first:

"Whether there were good grounds to believe the Lord and Lady guilty, and if not, they were then to inquire after the authors of the conspiracy."

The same instructions were afterwards produced to the Lords, both as evidence of the King's care and impartiality, and also as proof of the Commissioners' diligence in this business.

Lady Somerset, who was tried first, gave her judges but little trouble. Great as had been her position, brilliant as were her surroundings, to this young and beautiful, but most erring and passionate woman, life had early lost its charms. She was sated both with its pleasures and its crimes, and when placed on her trial at once pleaded guilty.

The next day, May 25th, her husband, Lord Somerset, was placed at the bar, and after a trial that lasted twelve hours, his peers pronounced the verdict of guilty.

The Lord Chief Justice considered himself entitled to, and, indeed, gained much credit from the nation generally, for the zeal and acuteness he had displayed throughout the whole progress of this terrible and mysterious affair; but though the King had expressed himself with such vehemence when commanding the matter should be thoroughly sifted, from the period of this trial Sir Edward fell into disfavour, both with His Majesty and with all the Royal favourites.

From this moment they, one after another, endeavoured to accomplish his ruin. They seized every opportunity of misrepresenting his conduct to the King, and as, unfortunately for the Chief Justice, serious disputes had arisen both in the Court of Chancery and in the Court of King's Bench, the proceedings of Coke were impugned on all sides.

His arrogant temper, his haughty manner of speech, the intolerance he displayed to all who might presume to differ from him, made him many personal enemies, and created around him a very army of foes.

The very fact, also, of his being so able a lawyer, so consummate a master of his profession, did but increase the rancour of those whom he had so haughtily rebuffed.

In all such encounters he almost invariably proved he was right both in law and in fact, and then the bitter words of his scorn stung the vanquished like a whip of scorpions.

There were very few persons, therefore, who would not rejoice in his humiliation and his fall; but amongst his many opponents, the most inveterate, the most powerful, and the most rancorous, was Lord Villiers, afterwards Duke of Buckingham.

Sir Edward had opposed with no small decision some matter that concerned the favourite's imperious will and pleasure, and Villiers exerted to the utmost his powerful influence to ruin the Chief Justice.

These intrigues resulted in Coke's being suspended from his office on June 30th, 1616. Sir Randolph Carew was commissioned to go Circuit, and in the following November, Sir Henry Mountague received the appointment of Lord Chief Justice.

It was during this enforced retirement from Court and public life, that Sir Edward Coke's higher qualities exhibited themselves in their most favourable light, and he showed the world with what calmness and courage he could support adversity.

The dignity that his vehemence had so often endangered during the days of his prosperity, now in the hours of adversity never failed him; and however bitter and undeserved the attacks made upon him, he either passed them over without notice, or replied to them in words of calm moderation.

His many legal works, his many letters to friends at this period, indicate with what resignation, nay, even with what content, he bore the loss of the power that had been so dear to him. Both his actions and his words testify how cheerfully he contemplated the end of all his ambitious projects, and looked forward to a life of complete retirement.

But so admirable a lawyer, so able a judge, was not destined to be long unemployed.

After his disgrace, men of far inferior talent had been placed in high stations; but ere much time had elapsed it soon became evident that the new Ministers and judges were unfit for the places to which they had been appointed.

When the ship is in danger or in a difficult position, the best pilot, however disagreeable he may be, must be called to the helm; and thus even those who had been most active in bringing about Sir Edward's fall, found it to their own interest to smooth the way towards his restoration to the King's favour.

For some time there had been serious differences amongst the Ministers, and at length the quarrel between the Lord Keeper Bacon and Mr. Secretary Winwood rose to such a pitch that they refused to sit in Council together.

It was at this juncture that the aid of so talented a man as the late Chief Justice was imperatively needed.

Unhappily, Coke was not content to let matters take their course, and to remain quietly on the pedestal he had so deservedly gained for himself, namely, to rest on his great reputation of being the soundest and most skilful lawyer in the United Kingdom. He thought to strengthen his position by an alliance with the family of the still powerful favourite, the Earl, afterwards the Duke of Buckingham, the famous "Steenie." For this purpose he negotiated a marriage between his youngest daughter by his second wife, Lady Hatton, and Sir John Villiers, the Earl's eldest brother.

Lady Hatton, a proud, violent woman, who was incessantly insulting and quarrelling with her husband, professed the greatest indignation that their daughter should be disposed of in marriage without her (Lady Hatton's) will and pleasure having been consulted in the matter. She forthwith, therefore, carried off the young lady, and shut her up in Sir Edmund Withipole's house, near Oatlands.

Sir Edward Coke, highly incensed that his authority should be thus set at naught, wrote to Lord Buckingham, requesting him to procure immediately, from the Privy Council, a warrant that would enable him to regain possession of his daughter. Unfortunately, before the warrant could be conveyed to him, he had learnt where Miss Coke was, and, with his usual impetuosity, without waiting for legal powers, he and his sons proceeded to Sir Edmund Withipole's house and took the young lady away from thence by force.

Upon this imprudent action, Lady Hatton, who, by her letters, appears to have been beside herself, so frenzied was she by rage, not only appealed to the Privy Council, but, by her personal entreaties, gained over the Lord Keeper Bacon to her side, he, probably, being nothing loth to have again an opportunity of attacking his old enemy.

Buckingham, however, was not a man to brook contradiction, and both he and his mother, Lady Compton, treated the Lord Keeper with extraordinary rudeness. Bitterly angry, the latter appealed to the Star Chamber, and also filed an information against Sir Edward Coke.

Thus this foolish marriage became a State business, and for many months the war of words and of law processes raged with exceeding fury. As might have been expected, the favourite eventually had his way, and, somehow or other, the two ladies who had been foremost in the fight. Lady Hatton and Lady Compton, came at length to a good understanding.

The marriage, therefore, was arranged. Sir Edward Coke was admitted to the presence of the King, and made a member of the Privy Council.

On the Michaelmas Day following, Sir John Villiers was married to Mrs. Frances Coke at Hampton Court, with all imaginable splendour.

Sir Edward's plans had succeeded. He had been restored to the King's favour, he had married his daughter to the brother of the Royal favourite; but he paid dearly for these triumphs. Not only had he to bestow on his daughter the sum of £10,000, to be paid down in money on the day of the marriage, but he had to assure to Sir John Villiers a rent charge of 2,000 marks per annum during his (Sir Edward's) life, and another one of £900 during Lady Hatton's life.

He engaged, also, to settle the manor of Stoke, in Buckinghamshire, a property he had destined for his other two daughters, on Sir John and Lady Villiers and their heirs.

Lady Hatton also had from her private fortune, which was considerable, to make large settlements upon her daughter.

Lady Hatton, who, by her own showing, must have been an intolerable woman, self-willed, passionate, and overbearing, had by this time become reconciled to her son-in-law and his friends; but she still pursued her quarrel with her husband with unrelenting acrimony.

Many letters still in existence testify to the heat and resentment of both parties. At length the dispute became quite a public matter, many persons of consideration interesting themselves keenly on one side or the other.

So fiercely did the warfare rage between all the partisans, that at one time Lord Houghton (formerly Sir John Hollis) was committed to prison for having, in conjunction with Lady Hatton, framed some scandalous libels respecting Sir Edward Coke.

This most disagreeable and trying wife seems to have lost no opportunity of insulting her husband both by word and deed. One of her means of annoyance was to give costly entertainments to the King, the Duke of Buckingham, and the whole Court, ostentatiously omitting her husband.

Not only was happiness far from this divided and discordant household, but the fluctuations in Sir Edward's fortunes were frequent.

During the early session of 1621, important matters occupied the attention of the House of Commons; liberty of speech, the increase of Popery, and many popular grievances were eagerly debated.

Sir Edward spoke strongly and warmly on all these questions, and his speeches are much commended by Camden. However, his views were not those either of the Court, nor of the favourite, and were indeed so ill received by the Government, that at the end of the year Coke was committed to the Tower; his chambers in the Temple were broken open, and his papers were delivered to Sir Robert Cotton and Mr. Wilson for examination.

Soon after his committal, Sir Edward was charged with having concealed circumstances relating to the trial of the Earl of Somerset.

Notwithstanding the assertions of his enemies, nothing could be proved against him, so after a short imprisonment he was released from the Tower. He regained his liberty, but at the same time he was made to understand that he had signally incurred the Royal displeasure. He was turned out of the Privy Council, the King observing:

"That Sir Edward was the fittest instrument for a tyrant that ever was in England."

Posterity does not endorse this opinion, because His Majesty's indignant remark was called forth by Coke's having *resisted* an undue exercise of the Royal prerogative.

He was never again reconciled to the Court during the life of King James, and even when Charles I. came to the throne, efforts were made to keep him out of Parliament by pricking him for Sheriff.

Sir Edward objected, and successfully, that it would not be seemly in one who had held the great office of Chief Justice of England, to attend the judges at the Assizes.

He was subsequently elected Knight of the Shire for Bucks, and during the sessions of 1628, distinguished himself more than any other man in Parliament, by his bold and skilful arguments in defence of the liberty of the subject, by the energy with which he urged upon the Government the necessity that existed for the redress of many grievances, and by the strenuous support he gave towards maintaining the privileges of the House of Commons.

It was during this same Parliament that he did the greatest service to his country that was, perhaps, ever done by a private man.

He it was who proposed and framed the "Petition of Rights," and it was Sir Edward Coke also, who successfully vindicated the right of the House of Commons to proceed against any subject whatever, however exalted the position of that subject might be.

After the dissolution of this Parliament in 1629, Sir Edward retired to his country house at Stoke-Pogis, Buckinghamshire, and there he spent the remainder of his days.

Though his life was prolonged to the great age of eighty-six, he retained his marvellous memory to the last. Were a passage quoted from any of his favourite authors, he would remember and mention, not only the context, but often the page in which the words would be found, and on all legal matters he would bring forward the papers he had written on the subjects in question.

His industry in committing to writing everything that interested him was beyond example, and posterity will never cease to admire his learned and laborious works on the laws of this country.

He also wrote some religious pamphlets, for he loved much to study the great doctrines of Christianity. He especially delighted to dwell on the sublime teachings of Our Lord, and during his last years, when the interests of this life, with all its pains and pleasures, were rapidly fading away, he, like Cardinal Wolsey, frequently lamented that he had not studied Divine laws with the same care and earnestness that he had devoted to the consideration and thorough understanding of temporal laws.

Our Saviour's own prayer was the one he best loved, and the last faint words that were feebly murmured by his dying lips were:

"Thy Kingdom come. Thy will be done."

Sir Edward died September 3rd, 1634, in the eighty-sixth year of his age.

He left behind him a vast mass of manuscripts and writings of all sorts, amongst them his will, in which he disposed of his very large fortune in the manner he judged best, between his children and his descendants.

On the very day of his death his papers were seized and carried away by an order from the Privy Council. Amongst other valuable documents was this will, and it is a remarkable fact, as connected with the wills of great lawyers, that this will of Sir Edward Coke's was never again found, to the great prejudice and detriment of his family and heirs.

OTHER EMINENT LAWYERS.

In the long list of eminent lawyers who were members of Gray's Inn, are to be found the names of three of the Yelverton family: Sir William Yelverton, Justice of the King's Bench in 1443; Sir Christopher Yelverton, Justice of the King's Bench in 1602; and also his son, Sir Henry Yelverton, Justice of the Common Pleas in 1625.

Emblazoned on the glass of the great window in the Hall are the arms of Guido Fairfax, called Serjeant from Gray's Inn in 1463. Also those of John Ernelye, Chief Justice of the King's Bench in 1519; of Sir Anthony de Fitzherbert, Justice of the Common Pleas in 1522; with those of Lord Riche, whose son Robert, also a member of Gray's Inn, was, in 1618, created Earl of Warwick; of Justice Stamford, Justice of Common Pleas in 1554, and of Dr. Thomas Wilson, Secretary to Queen Elizabeth in 1577, and who ultimately succeeded Sir Thomas Smith as Secretary of State.

Amongst the most ancient escutcheons on the walls are those of Sir William Gascoigne, Sir John Markham, Chief Justice of the King's Bench in 1400 and 1462, Lord Burghley, Sir Nicholas and Sir Francis Bacon, Thomas Moyle, Reader of the Society in 1534, and in 1542 Speaker of the House of Commons, Thomas Cromwell, afterwards Earl of Essex, of Henry Cromwell, the second son of the Protector, and of Sir John Holt, Chief Justice of the King's Bench in 1689.

The following sketch of Lord Chief Justice Holt is given in the fourteenth number of the *Tatler*:

"He was a man of profound knowledge of the laws of his country, and as just an observer of them in his own person. He considered justice as a cardinal virtue, not as a trade for maintenance. Wherever he was judge, he never forgot that he was also counsel. The criminal before him was always sure he stood before his country, and, in a sort, before a parent of it. The prisoner knew that though his spirit was broken with guilt, and incapable of language to defend itself, all would be gathered from him which could conduce to his safety, and that his judge would wrest no law to destroy him, nor conceal any that could save him."

Sir John Fortescue, of whom mention has been made (an ancestor of the present Lord Fortescue), was Lord High Chancellor of England under Henry VI.

In 1430 he was made Serjeant-at-Law, in 1441, King's Serjeant. The following year he became Lord Chief Justice of the King's Bench, and soon afterwards was raised to the dignity of Lord High Chancellor.

But he lost all on the deposition of the King. He was ever faithful to his old master, and for many years, therefore, remained in exile with Queen Margaret, and her son, Prince Edward.

When the Queen and the Prince returned to England, Sir John Fortescue accompanied them, but soon after the decisive battle of Tewkesbury, he was thrown into prison and attainted with other Lancastrians.

He was, however, subsequently pardoned by Edward IV.

Sir John, who was a man of great learning and a sound lawyer, wrote many valuable legal works. One of these, entitled, "The Difference between an Absolute and a Limited Monarchy as it more particularly regards the English Constitution," has passed through many editions.

The last of these editions, with amendments, was published as late as 1719.

Another of Sir John's works is "A Commentary on the Politic Laws of England."

He also wrote many other works, some of which are still in manuscript. It is in these papers that he describes the customs and practices of the Inns of Court.

STEPHEN GARDINER.

Stephen Gardiner, Bishop of Winchester and Chancellor of England in the sixteenth century, was an able lawyer, a learned divine, and a shrewd statesman.

Few men have risen higher by mere force of ability, few men have suffered greater changes of fortune, few have been more magnified and commended, and few more insidiously disparaged and outrageously treated than this famous Prelate, not only during his lifetime, but also after his decease.

The accounts given of him by contemporary historians are so confused and contradictory, that it is difficult to arrive at any just conclusion with regard either to Gardiner's character and disposition, or to fathom his motives as a churchman, or his measures as a statesman.

Some writers, amongst others, Hall and Fox, describe him as a very "devil incarnate," of a most fierce and sanguinary disposition, delighting in bloodshed. They declare also that he was the principal inciter to all the cruelties practised during the reign of Queen Mary.

Others again, according to Pitt and Persons, assert that the Bishop of Winchester was a very "angel of light," being of a singularly mild and compassionate nature, and so tender was his heart that it was through his influence and exertions that so many Protestants escaped death.

All agree, however, that this celebrated man had great abilities, much learning, and also an amount of general knowledge considerably in advance of the age. He had, however, many failings, and some vices, and either the natural bent of his mind, or the dangerous condition of his position, induced him to adopt a policy so tortuous, that even now it is difficult to trace the motives of some of the wisest and best, as well as those of some of his most injudicious and apparently cruel actions.

He was born at Bury St. Edmund's, Suffolk, but the year of his birth as well as his parentage he ever held secret. Some believe his parents were very obscure persons; but Dugdale, a great authority in such matters, asserts that he was the illegitimate son of a prelate nobly descended and royally allied—namely, of Dr. Lionel Woodville, Bishop of Salisbury, and brother of Queen Elizabeth Woodville, consort of King Edward IV. Certain it is that for many years neither he nor his brother bishop, Bonner, born under the same circumstances, ever used the surnames by which they were afterwards known. One called himself Dr. Stephens, the other Dr. Edmunds, until Gardiner, on obtaining place, assumed the surname he has made so celebrated.

At Trinity Hall, Cambridge, where he completed his education, Gardiner was early distinguished for his talents and his quick parts, especially for his extraordinary skill in Greek, and for the grace with which he spoke and wrote Latin. In process of time he applied himself to the study of Civil and Common Law, and his reputation both as a scholar and a lawyer speedily made him known to some of the famous men of that age.

He was first taken under the protection of a generous and powerful patron, Thomas, Duke of Norfolk, but soon afterwards was brought to the notice, and then received into the household of Cardinal Wolsey, as secretary to that great statesman, then in the zenith of his power. He was thus early initiated into the skilful yet dread policy that for so long a period made the powerful Cardinal the *de facto* ruler of this country.

A mere accident gained for Gardiner the favour of the King. Wolsey and the Emperor of Austria had been at one time such intimate friends that the latter, when writing (which he did frequently) to the Cardinal, always signed his letters with his own hand, subscribing himself, "Your son and cousin, Charles."

After the battle of Pavia, when the French King was taken prisoner, Wolsey unexpectedly changed sides, and from being a friend of the Emperor's, became a strong partisan of France's. This sudden change of sentiment may possibly have arisen from compassion, but Guiscard suggests another and less worthy motive.

Some months previously, and for some unexplained reason, the Emperor had ceased to write personally to the Cardinal, and only communicated with him through his secretary in the same manner as he did with other persons. According to Guiscard, Wolsey deeply resented this change and lapse of friendship, hence, therefore, his animosity.

Soon after the battle of Pavia, the Cardinal projected a treaty which was to change the aspect of affairs in all civilised Europe, which, indeed, it did. While this treaty was in progress, the King, coming unexpectedly to More Park, in Hertfordshire, found Gardiner busily employed in framing several of the important articles.

Few princes understood business or could transact it better than Henry; he rapidly, therefore, formed a favourable estimate of Gardiner's abilities. Not only did he appreciate the secretary's talents, but he was also pleased by his manner and conversation, and, above all, admired the fertility of invention of which Gardiner had already given convincing proofs. In short, Gardiner was the very man of whom the King at that moment had especial need.

Henry was bent upon obtaining his divorce from Queen Katherine; but though he had obtained many fair promises from Rome, he had failed to induce the then Pontiff, Clement II., to *do* anything towards advancing his suit. It was in the highest degree expedient, therefore, to send a delegate to Rome who was not only a wary diplomatist, but also a shrewd and skilful lawyer; above all, he must be one in whom the King could fully confide. In Gardiner were found all these essential qualifications, and the King did not hesitate to inform the Cardinal of the favourable impression his secretary had made.

With all his faults, there was nothing mean in the character of Wolsey. He was truly great in this particular, that he feared no man's rise, and grudged to none the reward due to talent. Though overbearing in temper, haughty in manner, tyrannical and revengeful in action, it was yet this noble quality that so strongly attached his adherents to him.

Far from viewing with displeasure the favourable impression made upon the King, he aided his secretary's interests with all his powerful influence; and in February, 1528, Gardiner, together with Dr. Fox, Provost of King's College, Cambridge, left England on a special mission to Rome.

It is evident, from many documents still extant, that the entire confidence, both of the King and of his Minister, had been reposed in Gardiner.

Respecting his conduct in Rome, historians are again at variance as to his motives; but all agree in praising his talents, his dexterity, and his diligence.

Some writers assert that he honestly endeavoured to carry out the King's and the Cardinal's wishes; others, on the contrary, maintain that, in order to secure his own advancement, he betrayed the Cardinal in this embassy, and that for this end he urged forward with the greatest eagerness proceedings which he knew his master in his heart desired might be spun out as lengthily as possible.

However, it must be admitted that such statements are barely compatible with the affection which Wolsey ever entertained for his secretary.

When writing to Gardiner, the Cardinal calls him "the half of himself, than whom none was dearer to him;" and in recommending him to the Pope, he says, when His Holiness hears him speak, it will be as if he heard the Cardinal himself.

At any rate Gardiner spoke boldly at Rome. His diligence and activity also were so great, that between the conflicting interests and exertions of the various Courts of England, France, Spain, and Austria, the unfortunate Pontiff was so pressed and harassed that he fell dangerously ill.

The perplexities of his mind seriously increasing the sufferings of his body, for some time he was like to die, a contingency that offered fresh occasion for the intrigues that were so rife at that period.

Had the Pope died, every effort would have been made to procure for Wolsey the suffrages of the Conclave; and at one time there appeared every probability that he would have succeeded to the Pontifical throne, but Clement recovered, and matters returned to their normal condition.

No sooner did the Pope's health enable him to transact business, than the matter of the English commission was again pressed forward. An extraordinary amount of care and skill were now required, not only to obtain the Pontiff's consent, but to pen the commission in such terms as would satisfy Henry, and dispose the Cardinal Legate Campegio to come to England with a good disposition towards the affair.

At length the important papers were obtained, and Fox at once forwarded them to the King.

The joy with which they were received by Henry, the Cardinal, and Anne Boleyn, was exceedingly great, and their satisfaction was expressed, not only by letters, but also by the valuable presents they made to the successful delegates.

To Gardiner, however, were allotted the greatest honours, for though Fox had nominally been the leading personage of the mission, yet Gardiner had in fact taken the chief part throughout the negotiations; and so impressed was Henry by the talents evinced by his clever agent, that the latter was speedily recalled from Rome, in order to be entrusted with the management of the case before the Legatine Court.

Indeed, so great at this time was the Secretary's influence, that without his advice the King was unwilling to commence his suit. No sooner had Gardiner arrived in England than he was made Archdeacon of Norwich, and soon after, the King took him from Wolsey's service and made him Secretary of State.

The suit had now begun; but whether Wolsey secretly sided with Rome in this matter, or whether he was only suspected by Henry of so doing, the King ere long became furious with his Minister on account of the delays that were for ever occurring to hinder the progress of the divorce.

The Pope's behaviour added much to the difficulties into which he was thrown; and believing that the Cardinal, while apparently aiding, was in reality fomenting the troubles by which he was beset, the King felt convinced that either he was being duped by his Minister, or that his Minister was allowing himself to be egregiously duped by the Court of Rome. In either case, Henry determined to trust Wolsey no longer, and only waited a favourable opportunity to effect his fall.

This opportunity soon presented itself. The successor who was needed was at hand, and again an accident furnished the King with the adviser that he so urgently required.

Dr. Cranmer, a tutor in the family of one Mr. Cressy, of Waltham Cross, was with his pupils at their father's house at Waltham, when the King with his Court passed a night there during one of the Royal progresses.

Drs. Gardiner and Fox were in attendance on His Majesty, and Cranmer had supper with them.

Men's minds were so occupied with the Royal divorce that little else was ever talked of; and the two courtiers, being already well acquainted with the great reputation for learning and solid judgment that Cranmer had gained for himself at Cambridge, sought to obtain his opinion on the matter.

Cranmer modestly declined to give an "opinion," but said that in his poor judgment it appeared to him that, if the marriage were unlawful, it was so by Divine precept; and if that were the case, then the Pope's dispensation could be of no effect either to confirm or annul it, for even the Pope could not make lawful that which God had declared to be unlawful. Instead, therefore, of continuing these long and fruitless negotiations with Rome, it might be better to consult all the learned men, or, indeed, all the Universities of Christendom, and then, according to their finding, the Pope must needs give judgment.

So much impressed were Gardiner and Fox by this advice, that the next day they laid the substance of it before the King.

Some writers say that Gardiner wished to make it appear that the opinion came from him, but that Fox, either from generosity to Cranmer or from spite to Gardiner, took care to mention from whence it was derived.

At any rate, these observations of Cranmer's caused him to be presented to the King, as Henry had at once perceived the importance of the suggestion thus thrown out.

Brilliant talents and an admirable judgment commanded respect, while the candour and uprightness of Cranmer's character secured for him the esteem of all who knew him. His rise in the King's favour was rapid, and honours were showered upon him.

In after times Henry might differ from his Minister, but he knew he need never distrust him. The King often said that the Archbishop of Canterbury (Cranmer) was the only Churchman he had ever known upon whom he could implicitly rely.

Unhappily, the haughty and hasty monarch occasionally succeeded in prevailing upon Cranmer to swerve from the strict line of wisdom and prudence to which his opinions inclined him, but although he yielded in action, the purity of his intentions and the honesty of his purpose were never doubted.

The new adviser's rapid advancement was the signal of Wolsey's fall.

While that powerful Minister was apparently enjoying the plenitude of his greatness, and triumphing in the magnificence of his position, destruction came upon him unawares. Great and brilliant had been his rise, equally great and fatal was his fall.

No sooner was his disgrace resolved upon than the Great Seal was taken from him, his vast possessions were confiscated, he was banished to his house at Asher, and informations were filed against him by the Attorney-General.

Such a tempest of misfortunes broke at once over the head of the unhappy man that his calamities seemed without end, and the ruin of his fortunes was speedily followed by the destruction of his health.

When great men fall, their pseudo friends of prosperous days fall away also. Such friendship but blossoms in the sunshine, it ever withers and dies when clouds obscure their sun.

In this time of cruel adversity, but very few of his many followers remained faithful to the once mighty Cardinal. Of these few the chief was his secretary, Thomas Cromwell, who proved his fidelity not only by his steady adherence to his master, but also by stoutly soliciting the Court in his favour.

As Cromwell's rank did not entitle him to admittance to the King's presence, he was compelled to have recourse to one of the Secretaries of State.

It was to Gardiner that he addressed himself, and it is to that Minister's credit that although, on account of Henry's hasty and tyrannical temper, the task involved considerable risk, the quondam secretary did not desert his old patron and master, but interceded for him with skill, if without much heartiness.

The unhappy Cardinal's letters at this time are most dismal. In one of them, to Thomas Cromwell, he says he has written it "with his rude hand and sorrowful heart," and he signs himself, "T. Carl[is.] Ebor misserrimus" (the most miserable Thomas, Cardinal of York).

Gardiner at this time was devoting himself to the difficult task of obtaining from the Heads of the Colleges and from the learned men belonging to the University of Cambridge, their declaration in the King's cause, a business that required no small amount of dexterity and artifice.

His efforts were successful. So brilliant an exploit must needs be rewarded, and his rise in the Church was rapid. In the spring of 1531, he was made Archdeacon of Leicester, and in November of the same year he was installed Bishop of Winchester.

"I have often squared" (meaning passed over) "with you, Gardiner," said the King, when he gave his Minister this valuable preferment, "but I love you never the worse, as the Bishoprick I now give will convince you."

The newly-made Bishop sat with Dr. Cranmer, then Archbishop of Canterbury, when that prelate declared Queen Katherine's marriage with the King to be null and void, May 23rd, 1533. He was then sent to Marseilles to intimate to the Pope and the French King, that in case difficulties should be made respecting the divorce, the King of England would appeal to a General Council.

On his return home he was called upon, together with all the other Bishops, to acknowledge Henry as Supreme Head of the Church; and his pen was henceforth constantly employed in vindicating Henry's proceedings, both respecting that monarch's divorce and subsequent marriage, and also with regard to his having thrown off the dominion of the See of Rome.

Gardiner's writings on these difficult subjects obtained for him at the time the highest reputation.

During this period of religious agitation, a strange spirit prevailed amongst all classes of people, of whatever denomination of religion they might be.

Though all needed tolerance, none would grant it. On the contrary, intolerance and bigotry seemed to rule every man's heart. Even those who, whilst they were themselves undergoing its sufferings, had groaned the loudest under persecution, were, when relieved, equally loud in their opposition to the smallest indulgence being extended to those who differed from them in opinion.

Whichever might be the party in the ascendant, its leaders were urged on to institute persecutions and trials, and to enforce executions whenever a doctrine was started to which they did not agree.

Some writers assert that Gardiner was vindictive and cruel; others, that he was forced tacitly to permit proceedings of which he disapproved, and of which he would willingly have mitigated the severity.

Others again say that the King's love of power, and his desire to show himself as a true son of the Church, although he had assumed her temporal headship, induced him to bear witness to his faith by severe measures, whenever her authority in doctrines was impugned by his subjects.

Certain it is, that now began a series of religious persecutions that cast shame and disgrace upon all who professed the name of Christ.

His holy Church on earth, far from being a tender mother to poor, suffering, and ignorant mortals, became a by-word for cruelty and bigotry, a very Moloch, who desired the sacrifice of her children both by fire and by the sword.

What can men deem are the chief attributes of the Almighty, that to give Him pleasure it is necessary to torture and put to death the children that His dear Son came to save?

It is sickening to read the list of those who suffered for religion's sake during the latter part of Henry's reign, and during the whole of the reign of his daughter, Queen Mary.

A Frenchman writing at this time from England, tells his friend in Latin:

"They have a strange way of managing in England, for those who are for the Pope are hanged, and those who are against him are burnt."

Henry also each year became more tyrannical and overbearing. He brooked neither opposition nor contradiction. His humours were so capricious that even his Ministers were constantly in personal danger, it being impossible to foresee how much involved the King might choose to consider them in the schisms that were being brought to the Royal notice.

Gardiner was certainly once in very considerable peril.

His young kinsman and secretary, Germain Gardiner, having been suspected of denying the King's supremacy, had been tried, condemned, and executed, and Gardiner's enemies sought to implicate the Bishop in his secretary's treasonable opinions.

Those who view Gardiner's character mercifully, urge that in order to secure his own safety and that of his relatives, he was driven into assenting rather than being a party to the numerous cruel executions that now sullied the history of this country.

Gardiner ultimately lost the King's favour, from having drawn up a paper of articles against Queen Katherine Parr.

It appears that, as usual, Henry had conceived some jealous suspicions of his Queen, and had directed the Bishop of Winchester to prepare these statements against her.

This important document having been confided to Chancellor Wriothesley, in order that the Queen should be committed to the Tower, he by accident or design let it drop from his bosom. It was picked up by a friendly hand, and immediately conveyed to the Princess.

Katherine so wrought upon the King's affection, that she not only succeeded in allaying his jealous fears and quieting his suspicions, but she also so excited his resentment against the writer of the accusations against her, that from that day Henry would never again see Gardiner.

It is also believed that this incident was the cause of the Bishop's name not being included in the list of the King's executors.

At one time, so high did Gardiner stand in the King's estimation, that Henry had resolved not only to nominate him as an executor, but also to direct that he should be a member of the Council to whom would be entrusted the executive power during the minority of his son.

Here again, however, is difference of opinion amongst historians, some writers asserting that it was not the animosity of Queen Katherine Parr, but the friendship of the Duke of Norfolk and his family, that proved the ruin of Gardiner's fortunes at this period.

Henry having become jealous of that powerful noble, seized upon every opportunity of humbling his relatives and friends.

But this, as well as most of the events of Gardiner's life, have been related by contemporary writers with such violence of partisanship, that it is difficult to ascertain the truth.

To Gardiner, however, must be assigned the merit that both during the life, and after the death of the King his master, he ever spoke and wrote of him in terms of much deference and respect.

Upon the accession of Edward VI. Archbishop Cranmer laboured earnestly to establish the great work of the Reformation on a firm basis, and was very desirous to obtain Gardiner's assistance, or, at any rate, his concurrence in his plans.

But this wily prelate would neither concur nor disagree with Cranmer's schemes. His ruling maxim had ever been to keep things quiet, and he asserted that this could not be done were any great alterations made either in Church or State.

He agreed in the wisdom with which the Archbishop sought to establish the Reformed religion, and also in his desire to do away with superstitious practices, but he saw grave objections to the innovation being attempted at present.

The King's youth and feeble health, the necessary absence of the Protector Somerset, who was detained in Scotland by military duty, made the future not only doubtful, but gloomy; and Gardiner was of opinion that it would be injudicious to disturb the present Church government.

However, Cranmer carried his point in so far as having a Royal Commission appointed for the purpose of visiting each diocese.

The Bishop of Winchester, notwithstanding his love of peace, opposed this measure, and refused to allow the Commissioners to enter his diocese. For this contumacy he was committed to the Fleet Prison.

His imprisonment there was not severe, the Warden of the Fleet being his friend, neither did it last long, and when released he returned to his diocese, and addressed himself zealously but quietly to his duties there.

This calm, however, was not of long duration, for within the year he was summoned to preach in London on St. Peter Day, and his doctrines so offended the Council that he was sent to the Tower where he remained a prisoner during the remainder of Edward's reign.

After Edward's death, Somerset visited Gardiner in prison with a view of effecting his release.

Gardiner readily expressed his approval of all that had been done to establish the Reformed religion, and promised for the future obedience to Royal authority, but he would not acknowledge that he had been guilty of contumacy in the past. On this point he was immovable, protesting that he was innocent in every respect.

He was brought before the Privy Council, and then three months were given to him for reflection.

When this period had expired, as the Bishop remained in the same sentiments, it was resolved to proceed judicially against him in order to deprive him of the See of Winchester.

He then refused to sign the articles that had been sent him previously, and to which he had in a measure assented, and he vehemently demanded to be tried as to the grounds of his imprisonment.

But the Privy Council refused his prayer, and his bishopric was sequestrated.

All these proceedings were much censured as being contrary to the liberties of Englishmen, and contrary also to all forms of legal procedure. It was thought very hard that a man should be put in prison solely from a complaint having been made against him, and still more hard that after two years' durance, and without further inquiry, articles should be put to him for his signature.

Such actions were quite indefensible upon any constitutional principles.

Archbishop Cranmer greatly deprecated this illegal harshness, for he foresaw the injurious consequences.

Such ill-timed severity would inevitably drive men like Gardiner, Tonstall, and Day, who had already acknowledged the King's supremacy, back to the Church of Rome, and the progress of the Reformation must thereby be sorely hindered.

And so it proved.

During the few remaining years of Edward's life, Gardiner remained in the Tower, a prisoner, and yet not strictly kept, for during this period he wrote many controversial pieces, and several Latin poems, besides putting into verse some of the most beautiful and poetical passages in the books of Ecclesiastes, Wisdom, and Job.

On the 3rd August, 1553, Queen Mary made her solemn entry into the Tower, when Bishop Gardiner, for himself, and also in the name of his fellow prisoners, the Duke of Norfolk, the Duchess of Somerset, Lord Courtney, and others of high rank, delivered a congratulatory speech to Her Majesty, who at its conclusion gave them their liberty.

On August 8th, he, with Archbishop Cranmer, and in the presence of the Queen, performed the obsequies of the late King Edward VI. The young monarch was buried in Westminster Abbey, and the ceremonial was the English funeral service.

The next day Bishop Gardiner again took possession of Winchester House, Southwark, after an imprisonment of rather more than five years. On the 23rd, he was declared Chancellor of England.

On the 1st October he had the honour of crowning the Queen, and on the 5th of the same month he opened the first Parliament of her reign.

He was also again restored to his academical honours, and was re-elected Master of Trinity Hall.

Not only were distinctions and emoluments thus showered upon him, but the esteem that the Queen manifestly had for him, and the confidence she reposed in him, led to his being speedily endowed with an unusually large share of civil as well as ecclesiastical power.

Mary was exceedingly anxious on three points.

The first was to substantiate the legitimacy of her birth by annulling her mother's divorce; the second was to effect the restoration of the old religion in England, and to reconcile this country to Rome; and thirdly, she eagerly desired to obtain the consent of Parliament to her marriage with Prince Philip of Spain.

In all these difficult and important matters Bishop Gardiner aided her with marvellous sagacity and unflagging zeal.

Thus it came to pass that the same man who procured the divorce for the father, obtained for the daughter the reversal of that divorce.

Now it was, in these days of triumph and success, that Gardiner gave evidence of his ambition, and of his time-serving nature. To preserve his ascendency over a weak and obstinate woman, he allowed himself to yield many points of which he disapproved, and then, having begun to swim with the stream, he found himself compelled to go faster and farther than he had intended.

The Spanish match was as distasteful to him as it was to the bulk of the nation, foreseeing, as he did, that it would involve this country in great expense, and that it would not tend to increase either the happiness or the good disposition of the Queen.

Unhappily, Mary had inherited obstinacy and violence of temper from her father, and a jealous and melancholy temperament from her ill-used mother.

All the early years of her life had been overshadowed by misfortune and insult, and she had been taught to believe that her sorrows mostly arose from the sinfulness of the nation in resisting the authority of the Church to which she belonged.

Unattractive in mind as well as in person, she loved a man who cared but little, if at all, for her, who had only consented to the marriage from motives of policy, and whose morose and sullen manners embittered the rare visits he accorded to his wife.

However great were Gardiner's errors, not only as a religious bigot, but as an unscrupulous and ambitious statesman, it must be remembered to his credit, that he was ever zealous in preserving what he deemed the constitution of his country, especially so in guarding her from the encroachments of foreigners.

To preserve his own power, he yielded against his judgment to the Queen's desire for her marriage with Philip of Spain, but in drawing up the articles of the marriage contract he took care so to frame them, that they would not only be passed easily by the English Parliament, but also that the Spaniards should be entirely excluded from any share in the Government of England.

To Philip was granted the "Title" of King of England, and his likeness was to be united to that of the Queen upon every coin and seal, but Mary's signature alone sufficed to give authority to all deeds and acts.

No Spaniard could hold office in this country.

The Queen could not be obliged to leave England, nor any child, should there be children, without the consent of Parliament.

The Queen was to have a jointure of £40,000 a year from Spain, and £20,000 from the Netherlands. Should the Queen have only daughters, they were to succeed to her throne, and have from Spain the usual portions of kings' daughters.

Should Philip survive the Queen, he was to have no share in the English Government.

Such stringent conditions appeared very disadvantageous to Spain; but so great was Philip's desire to obtain a foothold in England, that he yielded every point, believing, probably, that when once firmly established in this country, his own influence, combined with the power of the Church of Rome, would overcome much opposition and enable him to gain important concessions.

Parliament passed the Bill, and all obstacles to the marriage being now removed, King Philip, attended and accompanied by a magnificent suite of nobles, and escorted by a large fleet, put to sea, and arrived at Southampton at the end of July, 1554.

From thence he proceeded to the Palace at Winchester, where he was magnificently entertained by the Bishop. The following day he was solemnly married to the Queen by that prelate in the Cathedral of Winchester.

The newly-married pair made their entry into London with every circumstance of pomp and splendour.

At Windsor the King was installed a Knight of the Garter, and whenever he and the Queen appeared in public they were received by the people with universal acclamation.

But this pleasant and joyful state of things was not to be of long duration.

Philip speedily gave evidence of the distaste he felt for his bride, who, poor woman, had not only the misfortune of having an unlovely and unlovable countenance, but was also afflicted with a peevish and jealous temper. She was well aware how little attractive she was, and therefore suspected and disliked every woman who approached her. Her half-sister and heir, Elizabeth, was especially the object of her jealous fears.

This Princess, however, behaved with so much prudence and fortitude that she gave no loophole for the attacks of her enemies. Still, despite her care and prudence, and through the machinations of Gardiner and Cardinal Pole, she was sent to the Tower; but she was saved from perhaps a worse fate by her brother-in-law, Philip of Spain, who interceded in her behalf.

There is much reason to believe that of the two Philip much preferred the younger sister, and as Queen Mary was in bad health and her life most precarious, he hoped to marry Elizabeth after his wife's death.

The unhappy Queen, in the bitter disappointment occasioned by her marriage, again turned to her Church for consolation, and in spite of the King's and the Chancellor's opposition, insisted upon Cardinal Pole's coming to England, armed with a license under the Queen's Great Seal to exercise his functions as the Pope's Legate.

Soon after Pole's arrival, the Houses of Lords and Commons presented a petition to the King and Queen, praying that the nation might again be received into the bosom of the Catholic Church.

The Cardinal, after a lengthy oration, granted the petition, absolving the people of England, and declaring them reconciled to the See of Rome.

But the joy attendant on this proclamation was speedily troubled by the revival of the sanguinary laws for the repression of what was now called heresy.

These laws were speedily carried into execution with much rigour, and a bloody persecution was set on foot in almost all parts of the kingdom.

Whether this persecution was actively concurred in, or only passively submitted to by the Bishop of Winchester, is a matter of doubt. On one side he ever showed himself of the popular opinion by siding with Cardinal Pole when they sat together on various commissions. On the other hand, he saved the lives of many Protestants by merely locking them up until quieter and more peaceable days should come.

These were indeed dismal and dreadful times. A frightful religious zeal prevailed in the minds of men, inducing them, under colour of promoting the Gospel, to act precisely contrary to its spirit.

Gardiner, no doubt, had his share, and a large one, in these barbarous proceedings; but the whole reproach of these savage cruelties must not rest upon his memory.

It is certain that when there were hopes of an heir to the throne, the Chancellor induced the Queen to restore several prisoners to liberty. He went in person to the Tower on January 18th, 1555, and released the Archbishop of York, Sir Edward Rogers, Sir James Crofts, Sir Nicholas Throckmorton, Sir Edward Warner, Sir George Harper, Sir William Saintlow, Sir Gawin Carew, Sir Andrew Dudley, William Gibs, Cuthbert Vaughan, John Harrington, John Tremain, and others of less note.

It must not be forgotten, also, that during Mary's second Parliament, far from advocating the stringent laws that were in course of preparation against heretics, as persons of the Reformed religion were now called, he endeavoured to mitigate their severity; but in this, as in other matters, he was borne on by the stream of Royal and popular opinion, and, perhaps, compelled to acquiesce in proceedings of which he disapproved.

Thus Henry's severities and injustice were now emulated and surpassed by Mary's severities and cruelty.

If Gardiner disapproved in his heart of the persecution of heretics, his clemency or merciful inclinations did but little or nothing towards diminishing the frightful number of blazing piles that day by day consumed the bodies of miserable victims of religious fury.

Tortured by jealous love, unblessed with children, the unhappy Mary turned with increased fervour to religion as her only solace. Convinced, as she was, that the Church alone could afford relief to her sorrows, the bigotry of her nature and education demanded the holocaust of thousands of victims to appease the anger of an offended Deity.

Violent and obstinate, her Ministers, even had they wished to oppose her, could not, without peril to themselves, have resisted her stubborn resolution to have her way.

Unhappily then for England, her Ministers were both yielding and unscrupulous.

Not only was the Queen relentless in her resolve to exterminate heresy, but if the Bishop of Winchester relaxed in zeal, Bishop Bonner, and William, Marquis of Winchester (who for a time held the Great Seal), were eager to show their love for their Church by the torture they inflicted on her enemies.

Gardiner, whatever may have been his personal wishes, also yielded to the pressure put upon him; and by his dexterity and brilliant talents made himself of inestimable value to the Queen, and by so doing secured for himself supremacy in the Council, and also kept away other pretendants, especially Cardinal Pole, who was a formidable rival.

But if, as the writers who view him favourably assert, the Bishop of Winchester was thus impelled by the temper of his Royal mistress, and by a series of circumstances beyond his control, to acquiesce in actions of which he disapproved, what must be thought of the conscience of a man, who as statesman and Churchman permitted tortures to be inflicted, and executions to take place, that have made the reign of Mary a by-word of bloodshed and cruelty, and have covered the memories of this monarch and her Ministers with indelible disgrace?

The land was deluged in blood. The smoke of burning human beings darkened the air, as it rose in hideous sacrifice to the Almighty Father, and the shrieks of tortured victims, the prayers of martyrs at the stake, ascended daily to heaven in one great agonised cry for mercy—and for vengeance.

For a time England seemed as one stunned by the frequency of such unusual and horrible spectacles, but by degrees the mighty spirit of the nation was roused.

Laymen and Churchmen alike shook off their lethargy. The degrading cruelties of the reign of Catholic Mary placed Protestant Elizabeth more firmly on the throne; and when James II. struggled vainly to restore his Church to England, it was doubtless the remembrance of such scenes that induced many staunch Englishmen to welcome with enthusiasm the advent of the foreign Prince of Orange, and his English wife.

Fox, who describes Gardiner as a monster delighting in torture and blood, declares that the Bishop was stricken down by dreadful and deadly disease, the very day on which he had consigned Bishops Latimer and Ridley to the flames at Oxford.

This historian relates that the Duke of Norfolk came to sup at Winchester House, but that Gardiner would not sit down at table until the messenger from Oxford had arrived to say the sacrifice of the martyrs had been consummated.

As he joyed over the narrative of their sufferings, the hand of Heaven fell heavily upon him, and he died soon afterwards in inexpressible anguish of body and mind.

Other biographers say but little of the malady to which he succumbed, but Fox's account is clearly incorrect in many particulars. The Duke of Norfolk Fox alludes to, had been dead some thirteen months, and Gardiner made a speech in Parliament more than a week after the execution of these Bishops.

It is also a disputed point whether Gardiner really exhibited vindictive eagerness in bringing about the deaths of Latimer and Ridley, or whether, as some say, he endeavoured to save them, straining indeed his authority by offering Latimer a pardon without the knowledge of the Queen or the Council.

Bell, as well as Fox, declares that his death was a judgment brought on him for his cruelty to these martyrs, but Dr. Godwin, Bishop of Hereford, Dr. Fuller, and Archbishop Parker, all ascribe his death to natural causes.

For some years Gardiner had suffered from rheumatic gout, and ultimately consumption of the lungs was joined to his other diseases.

Whatever may have been his bodily ailments, it is agreed by every writer that his latter days were embittered by remorse and mental distress. The consciousness of his many sins of omission and commission pressed heavily on his mind. He constantly averred that having been endowed with much power, he felt that he had turned that power to evil rather than to good.

Some historians suggest that he repented having returned to the Church of Rome. Be this as it may, his opinions respecting the two Churches were such as to-day would be denominated broad.

His sermons were very remarkable, for eloquence, for talent, and also for a peculiar sophistry of argument, by which he could twist every quotation or opinion so as to suit the views he at the moment entertained.

His manner was earnest and noble, his voice impressive, and few could listen unmoved to the fervid accents, and to the brilliant and crafty reasoning by which he advocated the various points of his discourse.

It is evident, by the attachment that was felt for him for upwards of forty years, by some of the greatest statesmen in Europe, that he had the talent of conciliating men's minds and commanding their respect; and in his own diocese he was not only a wise and considerate Bishop, but he was infinitely loved and admired.

He died in Winchester House, London, but he was buried in Winchester Cathedral, close by the high altar.

The funeral was solemnised by an amount of pomp and magnificence rare even in those days, when much outward show was usual in every ceremony.

To conduct the unconscious dead to their last resting-place with every circumstance of lugubrious state and grandeur, was then deemed but fitting expressions of affection and respect on the part of the relatives and mourners.

Amongst the many cruel actions of which the odium has been cast upon Gardiner is the mournful tragedy of Lady Jane Grey. This poor girl was a victim to the political intrigues of an unscrupulous and ambitious party, and she paid by the sacrifice of her life, and that of her husband, Lord Guilford Dudley, for her brief and unwilling reign.

Sir Thomas Wyatt and Sir Peter Carew were the originators of a deep-laid and formidable plot, by which Mary and her sister were to be deprived of their rights of inheritance. They flattered the ambition of the Duke of Suffolk by suggesting that his daughter-in-law should ascend the throne, and thereby succeeded in implicating him and his children so completely in their projects that the heads of all ultimately fell upon the scaffold.

The alarm occasioned to the Queen and her adherents by the discovery of this plot was, no doubt, considerable; but against Gardiner is brought the grave charge of having fomented this panic, rather than having endeavoured to allay it.

But for his influence, the deaths of the principal conspirators, Wyatt and Carew, would have sufficed, and have been deemed a sufficient sacrifice. Many others amongst those who suffered in connection with the attempt might have been spared; but the Bishop is reported to have said:

"We may shake off the leaves and lop the branches, but if we do not utterly destroy the root, the hope of hereticks, we do nothing."

THE CHAPEL.

Amongst the many nooks and corners of this ancient Inn of Gray's, the little chapel must not be forgotten. Within its tranquil precincts all things speak of the past, for little has been changed therein for many generations.

Small and unpretentious as it is, few can enter this tiny place of worship without experiencing some emotion, without giving some thought to the many great and illustrious men—lawyers, Churchmen, and statesmen, now long numbered with the dead—who have knelt here for prayer and praise.

Centuries have elapsed since they have passed away, but their noble deeds and writings are still remembered and cherished.

Happily for England, this great race is not extinct. Some of those who now assemble within these walls have already made for themselves illustrious names— names that will be honoured and revered when they, in the fulness of time, depart; but others come here in sorrow, and perchance remorse, for many a promising but wasted life.

Poor, feeble mortals that we are! How many of us live but to exist; and often, indeed, that existence is but the puerile flutter of a day!

Truly, we are but as the sand upon the sea-shore. The tiny atoms shine, perhaps brilliantly, while the sun looks down upon them; but when clouds darken the sky, their brightness fades and soon is gone. Then a little later comes the rising tide—that overwhelming tide of Time, that sweeps them rapidly away. They are gone, and the place where they dwelt, and perchance glittered, knows them no more. No one asks for them; no one misses them. The sand is again as smooth as when they were there. The atoms around still quiver and shimmer in the sunshine as those now departed did of yore.

Not only from association with the past is the quiet little chapel attractive, but there is something soothing in its very aspect.

The fact that so little change has been made in the building or its arrangements for some hundred years is interesting, and it is touching to see the number of gray-headed men who usually attend the services. The memorials around also speak of those who are gone—the painted glass windows, the decorations, the richly-carved book of the Communion Service, are all gifts from those who dearly loved the old place.

In these days of greatly increased form, it is rare also to find a preacher who appears in the pulpit arrayed in the old black Geneva gown.

This quaintly-fashioned gown is precisely that to which our Puritan forefathers attached so much importance, deeming that it savoured less of Popery than any other raiment, inasmuch as its severe simplicity was as far removed as possible from the more imposing and, in their opinion, gaudy vestments of Rome.

From the pulpit in Gray's Inn Chapel may be heard sermons that stir men's hearts, that enlighten men's minds.

No man can hope to obtain the post of preacher to Gray's Inn, unless he possesses talents that entitle him to be listened to with respect and interest. Therefore, though quiet, though old-fashioned, though unemotional in ceremonies, many who think deeply, and who wish to listen to the words of those who also think deeply, may be found amongst the congregation gathered together in Gray's Inn Chapel.

The present little building stands upon the site of the ancient chapel that received its Royal license from Edward II. in 1314, when John, the son of Reginald de Grey, was authorised to convey thirty acres of land, two acres of meadow, and ten shillings rent, with the appurtenances, in Kentish Town, and in the parish of St. Andrew's, Holborn, to the Prior and Convent of St. Bartholomew's, in Smithfield, and to their successors, to provide a chaplain to perform divine service daily for the repose of the soul of the said John, and for the repose of the souls of his ancestors for ever.

The Prior of St. Bartholomew's, however, instead of providing a chaplain for the service of the chapel, appears, according to the accounts of the rents and payments of that monastery, to have paid the Society of Gray's Inn an annual sum of £7 13s. 4d.

When the monasteries were dissolved, Henry VIII. decreed that the Treasurer and Fellows of this same Society should receive yearly from the King's Highness, during the King's pleasure, the sum of £6 13s. 4d., to be paid in even portions, namely, at the "Feasts of The Natyvytie of Our Lord God, of the Annunciation of Our Blessed Ladye, the Vyrgyne, of the Natyvytie of Seynt John Baptist, and of Seynt Michaell, the Archaungell."

But in 1651, during the time of the Commonwealth, this payment ceased, and has never been revived, though during the reign of Elizabeth the officiating minister received a salary of £4 a year.

By an order of Pension, 15th November, 1598, it was ordered that the "Reader in Divinity" to be chosen, shall be a man unmarried, having no ecclesiastical living other than a Prebend, that he be without the care of souls, and that he shall keep the same place while he continues unmarried.

This order corresponds with an usage formerly existing with regard to the vergers of St. Paul's Cathedral, who, by one of the Cathedral statutes, were to be in a state of celibacy. They had either to relinquish their wives or their office.

According to Dean Milman, this statute declares: "That because having a wife is a troublesome and disturbing affair, and because husbands are apt to study the washes of their wives, or their mistresses, and no man can serve two masters, the vergers are to be either bachelors, or to give up their wives."

Since these times either wives have improved and become less troublesome, or else the vergers have become less subservient to them, for at St. Paul's this rule has been abolished. As regards the Reader of Gray's Inn, it still remains in force.

Unfortunately the chapel is, architecturally speaking, of no importance. It is low and insignificant, and quite unworthy externally of the venerable Inn to which it belongs.

Strype, in his edition of "Stowe," much praises the Hall of Gray's Inn, but laments that the chapel is so small, and wishes the Society would build a new one raised on arches, so that there would be a good dry walk underneath them in rainy weather.

The same writer mentions also a new entrance made into Holborn, where had been erected, he says:

"A fayre Gate and Gatehouse that were great improvements, making a more convenient and honourable passage, whereof this house stood in much neede, as the other entrances were rather posterns than gates."

To the shop beneath this gateway a certain interest is attached from its having been the place of business of Jacob Tonson, the celebrated bookseller, who removed here from Chancery Lane in 1697.

Several of the most ancient buildings were destroyed by fire in 1604, and unhappily also nearly all the earliest records of the Society perished in the same flames.

Subsequently the increasing number of students has necessitated the demolition of many more of the ancient houses, for some details respecting them that still exist, describe these old buildings as being not only dark and ill-convenient, but so deficient in space that the students had frequently to lodge double.

In 1688 the Inn appears to have been divided into three courts, but two of these have been thrown into one large area, called Gray's Inn Square.

This same lamentable fire of 1604 destroyed the greater part of the once valuable library. The present library contains about 13,000 volumes, a large proportion being, of course, works on law. There is also a small but valuable collection of manuscripts in twenty-four volumes, some of which are finely illuminated. They mostly relate to theological subjects, and date from the twelfth to the fifteenth century. One amongst them, Bracton's "De Legibus et Consuetudinibus Angliæ," in folio, written about the end of the thirteenth or beginning of the fourteenth century, was presented to the Society of Gray's Inn in 1635 by John Godbolt, then Reader of the Inn.

ARCHBISHOP LAUD.

Five Archbishops of Canterbury have been connected with Gray's Inn, one of whom was the celebrated Laud, Primate of England in 1633, temp. Charles I.; a man as much loved in domestic and private life for his kindness, charity, and tenderness, as he was feared, and indeed hated, as a Churchman and as a statesman, both on account of the rigid intolerance of his religious opinions, and from the uncompromising tenacity with which he strove to enforce every right to which he considered the Church entitled.

Unhappily, this unbending austerity, far from assisting, did but injure the cause he endeavoured to serve, and his zeal was so ill directed, that it eventually brought his head to the block, and was one great cause of the civil and religious war that for so many years desolated this land.

Animated as he was by the religious fervour of the times, Laud was inflexible in his resolution of forcing upon all men the adoption of principles he believed to be right. Even the fatal examples of previous reigns had not taught him that one of the noblest attributes of Christianity is forbearance. Great as was his pride, stern and severe as were his judgments, yet in many respects the Archbishop was a man to be much respected, even much loved. He considered that his pride as a Churchman was but a fitting attribute of the great position he held as Primate of England. He believed that his duty to the Church demanded of him sternness and severity in dealing with her enemies, and he evinced the heartfelt sincerity of his opinions by giving up his life in support of them.

When the end drew near, Laud nobly testified, by the fortitude and calmness with which he faced death, by the tender thoughtfulness he showed for all around him, that his pride and severity were but for his office, that he himself was, as he had ever been, a humble and sincere Christian.

He has been accused by his enemies of endeavouring to overthrow the Protestant religion; but one of the best pamphlets ever published against Roman Catholic tenets was written by Laud in his answer to Dr. Fisher. His foes also were especially rancorous against him for the attempts he made to introduce wholesome and lawful games on Sundays and holy-days; a proceeding viewed with much disfavour by the strict Puritans of the day, who held that all exercises on the Sabbath, save those of religion, tended to Popery.

Laud also endeavoured to restrain the publication of irreligious and other evil books, by subjecting all publications to the revision of the Star Chamber. This endeavour on the part of the Archbishop caused a storm of indignation, for it was held to be an attempt to subvert the existing laws, and to restrain the liberty of the people. The indiscreet zeal, also, that he displayed in his efforts to introduce into Scotland the Liturgy of the Church of England, made him many enemies in that country.

At length, after many years of energetic but fruitless struggles, his foes prevailed against him; he was committed to the Tower, tried before a committee of the House of Lords, and condemned to death.

He was beheaded on Tower Hill on the 10th of January, 1641, in the seventy-second year of his age.

Charles, it is said, though lamenting the death of his old servant, made no attempt to save the life of one who, though opinionated and mistaken, had served his King with affectionate fidelity.

Archbishop Laud's only sister married Sir John Robinson, afterwards Governor of the Tower in the reign of Charles II., and, if we may believe Pepys, an intimate friend and boon companion of that merry monarch. The descendants of Lady Robinson, namely, Sir George Robinson of Cranford, Northamptonshire, Lord Lyveden, of Farming Woods, Northamptonshire, and John Harvey, of Ickwell-Bury, Bedfordshire, still possess many interesting relics of this famous prelate.

BISHOP JUXON AND ARCHBISHOPS SHELDON & WHITGIFT.

Archbishop Dr. William Juxon was Bishop of London when King Charles I. was brought to trial, condemned, and executed.

Throughout the civil wars, Juxon had resided at Fulham, and although his steady adherence and loyalty to the King were well known, the prelate's meek and inoffensive behaviour and his many charitable works had gained him the respect of even the most violent of the Puritan and Republican parties.

When the trial of the Royal martyr commenced, Charles, who early foresaw its result, especially requested the attendance of Bishop Juxon; and the ministrations of this good man and truly Christian divine soothed the unhappy monarch during the terrible hours of his last days on earth.

Juxon was unwearied in his devotion to his Royal master. He attended the unhappy monarch on the scaffold; he received the last commissions, he alone heard the sufferer's last words.

When all was over, the Bishop, at considerable personal risk, took charge of the mortal remains and conveyed them to Windsor. When there, however, in spite of urgent remonstrances and earnest entreaties, he was refused permission by the then Governor, Colonel Whichcote, to perform the final sad offices over the Royal corpse.

On his return to London, Juxon was thrown into prison for refusing to divulge the particulars of his conversations with the King; but his imprisonment was not of long duration, and, when released, he returned to Fulham Palace, where he was allowed to pass several months in peace.

The following year, however, he was deprived of his bishopric. He then retired to his own property in Gloucestershire, where he resided in much privacy until the Restoration. He was then made Archbishop of Canterbury, and had the satisfaction of placing the crown upon the head of Charles II.

The Archbishop died in 1663. Few men have left this world more universally beloved than this excellent prelate; but few men have equalled him in having consistently led a life as blameless as it was self-denying—a life made beautiful by exceeding humility, gentleness, and charity.

He was succeeded in the archbishopric by Gilbert Sheldon, in 1677. This prelate had formerly been Clerk of the Closet to Charles I., and had ever adhered faithfully to the King during the troubles of the Rebellion and the trials of the Royalists during the Commonwealth. At the Restoration he was made Bishop of London, and subsequently became Archbishop of Canterbury.

Dr. Sheldon was a man of great learning and of an excellent life. His charities were numerous and magnificent, and he has also immortalised his memory by building the famous theatre at Oxford that bears his name.

Another Archbishop of Canterbury connected with Gray's Inn was Dr. John Whitgift, Primate of England in 1583. A man of very exceptional talent, eminent alike for the ability of his writings, and for his stirring eloquence in the pulpit.

By some historians he has been much praised, by others equally blamed; but it must be remembered that Whitgift lived at a period when men's minds were agitated and much troubled by religious and civil contentions, and the great prelate was a violent man amongst violent partisans.

He was especially noted for his bitter hostility both to the Roman Catholic party and to that of the Puritans. By each of these religious bodies he was therefore equally hated and dreaded, and in many instances his judgments and his actions were harsh and severe; still, it must also be remembered that at a time when the Church of England had to contend with many enemies, foreign as well as domestic, and was menaced with dangers unknown to us in these days, Whitgift held the reins of government with an able and a vigorous grasp, and to his credit it can be said that though severe he was never cruel.

This Archbishop was much favoured by Queen Elizabeth, and did many excellent works of charity, both establishing and assisting large hospitals for the poor.

In the east window of the chapel at Gray's Inn may be seen the arms of these prelates, as well as those of William Wake, Archbishop of Canterbury in 1716. Here, also, are the escutcheons of George Morley, Bishop of Winchester, Nathaniel Crewe, Bishop of Durham, and of Walker King, Bishop of Rochester.

Thus we see that this venerable Society exhibits, emblazoned on her ancient walls, the names and arms of those who, during their lives, shed such lustre on the sheltering house in which their earliest struggles were fought.

The children she had so much reason to be proud of honoured her in their lives. They have gone, but in death she cherishes their memory, and ever fondly and jealously guards their names from oblivion.

But now, farewell, pleasant old Inn, with all your glorious Past, your glorious Present, and your glorious Future.

The student, labouring hard to master the difficulties of the magnificent but stern profession of the Law, must often feel his heart stir within him with emulation, when he remembers how many are the celebrated men who have also studied diligently beneath the shelter of these gray old walls, or who have reposed, perchance, at times beneath the spreading branches of the grand old trees.

The gates of the Temple of Fame are open to every man, if he can but win his way up the steep and thorny path that leads to its golden portals.

None, however, can grapple with the difficulties of the road but the courageous, the resolute, and the talented.

Woe to him who lingers or faints by the way. To the laggard, as to the weakly, the shining temple becomes but a glittering mist. It is there, but unattainable. He who falters or shrinks from the struggle can but veil his head in grief and disappointment, as those aspirants who are made of stronger and sterner stuff than himself pass him in the race.

Centuries roll on, generation after generation passes away; but those who love this venerable and time-honoured Society, trust with heartfelt affection and gratitude that there will ever be some "Chronicles of this Old Inn."

THE END.

Lector House believes that a society develops through a two-fold approach of continuous learning and adaptation, which is derived from the study of classic literary works spread across the historic timeline of literature records. Therefore, we aim at reviving, repairing and redeveloping all those inaccessible or damaged but historically as well as culturally important literature across subjects so that the future generations may have an opportunity to study and learn from past works to embark upon a journey of creating a better future.

This book is a result of an effort made by Lector House towards making a contribution to the preservation and repair of original ancient works which might hold historical significance to the approach of continuous learning across subjects.

HAPPY READING & LEARNING!

LECTOR HOUSE LLP
E-MAIL: lectorpublishing@gmail.com